D1372438

A WORLD
OF WHEELS

A World of Wheels

Cars 1990 to Present Days
Production goes World Wide

G. N. Georgano

Bengt Ason Holm

MASON CREST PUBLISHERS, INC.

A World of Wheels - **Cars 1990 to Present Days**

World copyright © 2002
Nordbok International,
P.O. 7095, SE 402 32 Gothenburg, Sweden

This edition is published in 2002 by Mason Crest Publishers Inc.
370 Reed Road, Broomall, PA 19008, USA
(866) MCP-BOOK (toll free).
www.masoncrest.com

Cover: Bengt Ason Holm

 2 3 4 5 6 7 8 9 10
Library of Congress Cataloging-in-Publication Data on file at the Library of Congress

ISBN 1-59084-489-0

CONTENTS

1
PROGRESS IN TECHNOLOGY

A comparison between the technologies of 1970 and 1990 shows tremendous progress in the fields of engines, transmissions, steering and suspension—yet most of the progress has been made during the last ten years. This is understandable when one remembers that the 1970s were nervous, defensive years for the world's motor industries. Fuel economy was paramount, and improved performance seemed irrelevant if not downright anti-social. The 1980s have also seen the industry on the defensive, largely against the charges of polluting the atmosphere, and this has also led to important changes in fuels and engine design.

Turbochargers—simple but very efficient!

The single most significant development in engine design has been the turbocharger, together with the limited return of its rival, the supercharger. The turbocharger principle is so simple as to surprise us that it was not adopted earlier. Patented in 1905 by a Swiss engineer, Alfred Buchi, it was not commercially applied to engines until World War II, when aircraft engine makers Allison and Pratt & Whitney began using turbochargers developed for them by Garrett AiResearch, a name famous today in the same field.

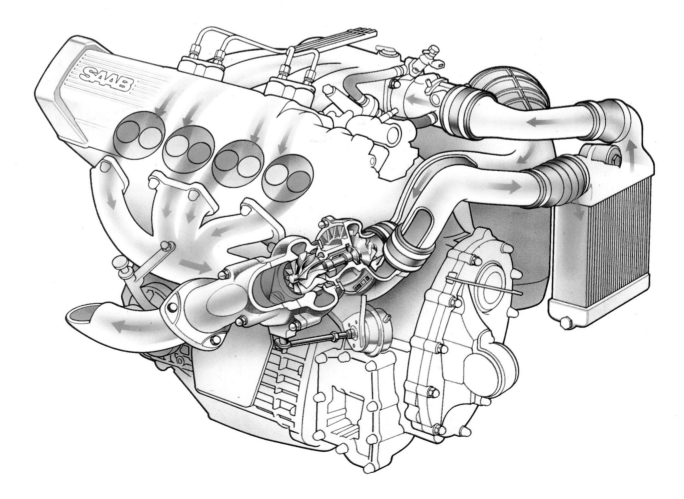

This is the engine that really started the turbo era: Saab's 2-litre four-cylinder turbocharged unit from 1978. Saab was not the pioneer, but made the name Turbo synonymous with that company—and the 99 Turbo, as well as the later 900 Turbo, sold very well in America. The original output of 145 bhp was raised to 175 bhp in the 16-valve version.

Here we see the intercooler (right side of engine) which cools down the hot, compressed air taken in from the turbo. The reason is that cool air occupies less volume than hot air, enabling more air to be pressed into the cylinders, and thus also more fuel which raises the power.

Buchi's device used a piston pump driven by exhaust gases, but all subsequent turbochargers have embodied a small centrifugal compressor and a radial-flow turbine mounted on a common axial shaft. Placed on the engine's exhaust manifold, the turbine is activated by the exhaust gases and drives the compressor, which forces air into the carburetter at a pressure greater than atmospheric. This boosts power output by up to 100%, using the exhaust gases which would otherwise be wasted. It is an example, rare in the engineering world, of 'something for nothing'–for unlike the supercharger, which embodied an engine-driven compressor, the turbo made no demands on the engine's power.

Chevrolet Corvair Monza was first

The first application of a turbocharger to an automobile engine was made by General Motors' Chevrolet Division, on their Corvair Monza Spyder of 1962. The Corvair was a controversial design anyway, with its rear-mounted air-cooled flat-6 engine, and the turbocharger came as part of a $317 package which included additional chrome, heavy-duty suspension and a multi-gauge instrument panel complete with rev counter.

The turbocharger differed from more recent thinking in that it was mounted between the carburetter and inlet manifold, drawing air through the carb, whereas modern turbos all blow air into the carb or fuel-injection system. Unrefined though it may have been, it raised the Corvair's power by more than 50%, from 95 to 150 bhp. Its discontinuation was due to the Corvair's controversial reputation for quirky handling, rather than to any defects in the turbocharger itself.

Soon after the turbocharged Corvair had appeared, GM's Oldsmobile Division also offered a turbo on their F85, with a V8 engine of 3+ litres. This was the same engine design that was later sold to Rover, being used in the SD1, Range Rover and Morgan Plus 8. The turbo operated in a similar way to the Corvair's, being mounted in the neck of the Vee, drawing the mixture through the Carter carburetter

above the left-hand cylinder bank. With a maximum boost of 6 psi, it increased the F85's power from 155 to 215 bhp.

Yet with certain grades of petrol, carbon deposits built up in the cylinder. Olds engineers tried to solve the problem by injecting a 50–50 mixture of methyl alcohol and water between the carburetter and turbocharger, but this proved unreliable, and the turbo was dropped after two seasons. However, to its credit and unlike the Corvair's, the Oldsmobile's turbo system incorporated a wastegate. This was in effect a safety valve which 'blew off' when pressure was too high and likely to damage the engine. All modern systems incorporate a wastegate, many having variable control to operate at different pressures according to engine speed.

BMW 2002–killed by the energy crisis

In 1969, BMW campaigned turbocharged 2002 saloons in the European Touring Car Championship, winning the 2-litre class. These were the first turbocharged cars to face a starting line, and four years later the makers offered the 2002 Turbo as a production car. With a KKK turbocharger and Kugelfischer fuel injection, the BMW was exceptionally fast for its day. A top speed of 130 mph from a two-door saloon of less than 2 litres capacity was phenomenal, but it was far from faultless. Turbo lag, the biggest drawback of the system, was certainly present, with a lapse of several seconds between flooring the accelerator and any response from the engine.

The turbo power was not really felt until engine speed reached 4,000 rpm–and when it did come in, it kicked violently. In addition, the system was not always reliable, and fuel consumption was only 19.5 mpg. Although owners who could cope with all this delighted in their 2002 Turbos, only 1,672 were sold in the 1973/4 seasons, and BMW have not offered a turbocharged car since. It had the misfortune to arrive just at the height of the energy crisis. Early models had the words 2002 Turbo in mirror-image writing on the front spoiler, but this was considered intimidating to other road users, and was quickly dropped. Perhaps if it had appeared a decade earlier or later, the BMW Turbo might have enjoyed a better fate.

A year after the BMW's demise, Porsche added the power of a turbo to their already very successful rear-engined 911. Because people expected a Porsche to be fast, this escaped the censure that had greeted the BMW, and it was a more satisfactory car anyway. The KKK turbocharger had a maximum boost of 11.75 psi, higher than the BMW, and raised output from the 2994-cc engine from 200 to 260 bhp.

Two years later, capacity was increased to 3229 cc and power to 300 bhp. This was due not only to the greater capacity, but also to the use of an intercooler. The latter functioned like a radiator, cooling the compressed air before it entered the engine, making it more dense and helping the engine to develop more power. Intercoolers had been employed in heavy diesel trucks for some years, but Porsche pioneered their use on passenger cars. There were three variations of intercooler: air/air, air/water and air/oil.

The BMW 2002 Turbo was exceptionally fast for its day, and the use of turbocharging raised its output from 100 to 170 bhp. Unfortunately the engine was unreliable and not up to normal BMW standards. It also had the typical early turbo problem of delayed power delivery. A press of the accelerator had no effect at first, then a shocking one.

Early cars had stripes with the text "Turbo" on the front spoiler. The letters were reversed so that a driver ahead would read them in a rear-view mirror and move aside.

Two representatives of the early turbo era, which made this innovation well-known to the ordinary car consumer, were the Porsche 911 Turbo (right) and the Saab 99 Turbo (below right).

The Porsche had a 6-cylinder boxer engine of 2993 cc, later 3299 cc. Output was 260–300 bhp and top speed was 160 mph, while the Saab was good for 125 mph.

Porsche and Saab make turbos their hallmark

So charismatic was the Porsche Turbo that, for a while, it was the car that most people automatically thought of when the word 'turbo' was mentioned. However, others soon appeared. The first manufacturer to use a turbo on an ordinary saloon car was Saab. Here the motive

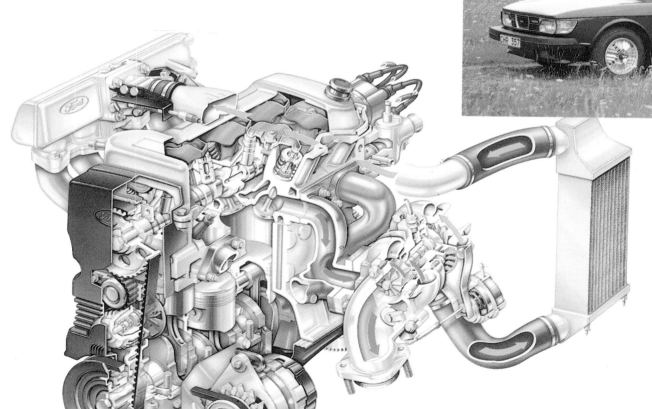

Saab chose turbocharging to maintain their car's performance in spite of emission-control regulations. First made in 1977, the 99 Turbo (above), with Garrett AiResearch turbocharger, had 145 bhp from its 2-litre engine, compared with 118 bhp from the normally aspirated version. Made in four saloon/hatchback models with two to five doors, it was the first successful turbocharged family car, and was followed by the turbo version of the larger-bodied 900.

Another company surfing on the turbo wave was Ford, who brought out the Escort Turbo in 1984. Illustrated (left) is a ghost-view of the 1.6-litre engine, which produced 130 bhp at 5,500 rpm.

was not so much to increase performance as to maintain it in the face of increasingly strict US emission laws. In the 1970s the response of American manufacturers had been to increase the size of the engine, but this was an option not available to Saab.

A 4-cylinder engine larger than their existing 1985-cc unit would have been too rough, and six cylinders were ruled out on the grounds of space and fuel consumption. The turbocharger was the answer, and was first seen on the 99 Turbo of 1977. It was made by Garrett AiResearch, the leading firm in the field in the USA and Europe, and was mounted ahead of the 45° slanted engine, close to the exhaust ports, with fresh air drawn in from the other side and the pressurized air returned also to that other side. With a maximum boost of 10 psi, the Saab's engine power was raised from 118 to 145 bhp, later going up to 175 in the 16-valve twin-cam engine used in the 900 cabriolet and 9000 saloons of the 1980s. The 99 Turbo was a highly significant car in that it was successful and mass-produced, unlike the flawed BMW and limited-production Porsche.

By the end of the 1980s, turbocharging had reached all engine sizes from the Mitsubishi Dangan ZZ (below), with 548 cc and 64 bhp, to the Bentley Mulsanne (right) with 6750 cc and 330 bhp. The Dangan (meaning a bullet) was a remarkable car with five valves per cylinder, 116 bhp per litre, and a top speed of 100 mph. It was the most powerful of all the Japanese minicars, which are restricted by law to 64 bhp.

Turbocharging helped restore the Bentley name to prominence. In 1982 only 6% of the cars built by Rolls-Royce carried Bentley badges, but by 1985 the figure had risen to 17.9% and in 1989 it was 49%.

The 1980s have seen a proliferation of turbos, and it has now become one of the standard methods of increasing power. For many the word 'turbo' on the boot lid was a necessary status symbol (although that arch-yuppie car, the VW Golf GTi, was not turbocharged), just as '16 valve' became a few years later.

Turbos have been applied to a wide variety of engine sizes, from the 548-cc 64-bhp Mitsubishi Minica Dangan ZZ to the 6750-cc 330-bhp Bentley Turbo R. The first turbocharged automatic transmission car was the Audi 200 Turbo of 1981 – and its cousin, the outstanding Audi Quattro, was also turbocharged. Other noteworthy cars to have enjoyed the turbo boost have included the Citroen CX25, Ford Escort, Sierra, Sapphire and Capri, Lancia Delta, Lotus Esprit (whose makers preferred to call their air/water intercooler a chargecooler), Toyota Celica, TVR and Volvo 760. Maserati's Biturbo, as its name implied, had two turbochargers, Japanese-built IHI units, one for each bank of the V6 engine. Renault used turbos on many of their models, from the 5 hatchback to the rear-engined Alpine GT coupé.

American slowness to adopt the turbo

After the false starts of Corvair and Oldsmobile in the 1960s, American manufacturers did not return to the turbocharger until the 1978 model year, when Buick brought out a turbo version of their 3.8-litre V6-engined Le Sabre Sport Coupe. This developed 165 bhp compared with 105 from the non-turbo unit of the same size. Buick dropped it after two years, but it was used by Chevrolet in 1980 and 1981 on their Monte Carlo coupé, and Pontiac offered a turbocharged V8 in the 1981 Firebird Formula and Trans Am models.

Ford turned to the turbo on the 1979 Mustang. This used a single-overhead-camshaft 4-cylinder engine related to the European Ford 2-litre units. The Garrett turbocharger, initially without intercooler, boosted power from 88 to 116 hp. Not very inspiring, but power was upped to 140 bhp for 1983, and to 175 bhp on the intercooled SVO coupé of 1984.

The final development of this engine/turbocharger combination produced 200 bhp, but it was dropped after 1986. This engine was used in Ford's Thunderbird from 1982, and gave the sleek coupé a top speed of 138 mph by 1987, making it faster than the same car with a 4.9-litre normally-aspirated V8 engine. For 1989 the turbo was replaced by a supercharged V6 engine which gave smoother and more progressive power delivery.

The Chrysler Corporation also adopted turbocharging in the 1980s, on the transverse-engined front-wheel-drive Chrysler Laser and Dodge Daytona coupés. The 2213-cc single-overhead-camshaft engines gave 146 bhp in their original 1983 forms, increased to 174 when

The Dodge Daytona (above), based on Chrysler's K-car, was delivered in two basic versions: the standard one with a 2.2- or 2.5-litre engine, and the Turbo Z with the 2.2-litre unit. The latter could be bought with a so-called CS-Handling Package for better roadholding.

The Chrysler Maserati TC convertible (left) was based on the LeBaron and used the same turbocharged 2213-cc 4-cylinder engine, but with a twin-overhead-camshaft 16-valve head designed by the Italian company, which raised output by 31 bhp to 205 bhp. Seen as a competitor for the Cadillac Allante, it was considerably cheaper at $33,000 compared with $57,000.

12

The Maserati Biturbo displayed the first use of twin turbos in a series-produced car. With twin IHI exhaust turbos, the 2.5-litre engine developed 188 bhp at 5,500 rpm.

The Citroen CX (left) could be had with either a normally turbocharged petrol engine or a turbocharged diesel engine. The latter's output was raised from 75 to 95 bhp by using a turbo. Shown here is a 1985 Citroen CX GTi. The CX model was built between 1974 and 1989, yet the estate model has survived into the 1990s.

an intercooler was used from 1987. This gave the Dodge Daytona a top speed of 137 mph. Turbochargers were also used in the Chrysler-Maserati, launched in 1986. This used the same block as the Daytona, but had a twin-overhead-camshaft 16-valve head designed by Maserati, which gave 205 bhp.

Turbocharged diesel engines were first seen on heavy trucks in the 1960s. When small diesels were adopted for passenger cars in the 1970s, the turbo was seen as an obvious way to raise specific output to something comparable with a petrol unit.

A typical application was the 2.4-litre turbo diesel made by the Italian VM company and supplied to, among others, Range Rover. This had four individual cylinder heads, a compression ratio as high as 22:1, and a maximum boost pressure of 12 psi from the intercooled KKK turbocharger. Output was 112 bhp, which compared well with the 128 bhp delivered by the larger 3528-cc V8 petrol engine also fitted to the Range Rover. Without the turbo, a 2.4-litre diesel would barely have delivered 80 bhp. Other companies who offered turbo diesels by the end of the decade included Citroen (BX and CX), Fiat (whose

This cutaway drawing shows the construction of the Fiat Croma turbo engine, which had a swept volume of 2445 cc. The output was 55 bhp with a standard diesel version, or 74 bhp with turbocharging.

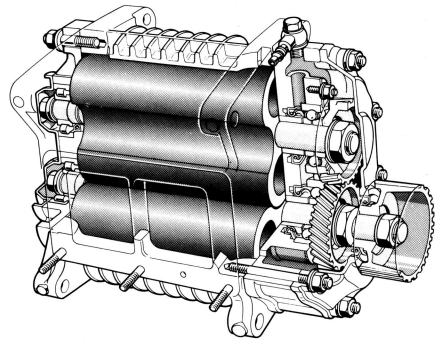

The year 1983 saw the return of the supercharger. First out was Lancia with the new Trevi Volumex VX, a positive-displacement compressor of Roots type. This unit was put into the Lancia Beta, but was expensive and thus dropped after only two years. With an engine of 1995 cc, the supercharger raised the output from 122 to 135 bhp, really not much compared to what was possible with a turbocharger.

2445-cc unit featured direct injection as well), Mercedes-Benz, Peugeot (405 and 505), Renault (21 and 25), Toyota, Volkswagen (Golf and Jetta), and Volvo.

The return to superchargers

Although the turbo achieved widepsread success in the 1980s, it suffered from the inevitable drawback of lack of boost at low engine speeds, leading to the notorious 'turbo lag' which bedevilled all models to a greater or lesser extent. The turbo could not begin to work until the engine was pumping out exhaust gases at a reasonable rate. There was no effect at a turbo speed of 10,000 rpm, and only a little at 40,000, while a really useful effect did not arise until over 80,000 rpm. (The highest speed of a modern turbocharger such as the Garrett T3 is up to 190,000 rpm.)

The supercharger, on the other hand, which had a history dating back to the 1920s, was a compressor directly driven from the engine by belt, chain or gears, and so delivered its boost in direct proportion to engine speed. Its appeal lay in the high outputs that could be extracted from a small displacement, such as the Formula One cars of 1½ litres in the early post-war years, although there were large supercharged engines such as the '4½-litre blower Bentley' and the 7-litre Mercedes-Benz SS and SSK.

However, improved breathing and a reduced obsession with small engines made the supercharger obsolete by the 1950s, and it seemed

to have disappeared completely. Its drawback compared with the turbocharger was that it absorbed some of the engine's power, up to 10 %, thus partially defeating its object. Yet recent research has indicated that the turbo also reduces efficiency to a greater extent than was originally thought, by obstructing the free flow of the exhaust gases.

This has led to a revival of interest in the positively-driven supercharger, which was tried on the Lancia Beta Volumex in 1983. The 1995-cc twin-cam engine gave 122 bhp in normally aspirated form, and 135 bhp with the Roots-type supercharger, which was less of an increase than would have been achieved with a turbo. The Volumex was expensive, and it was dropped after two seasons.

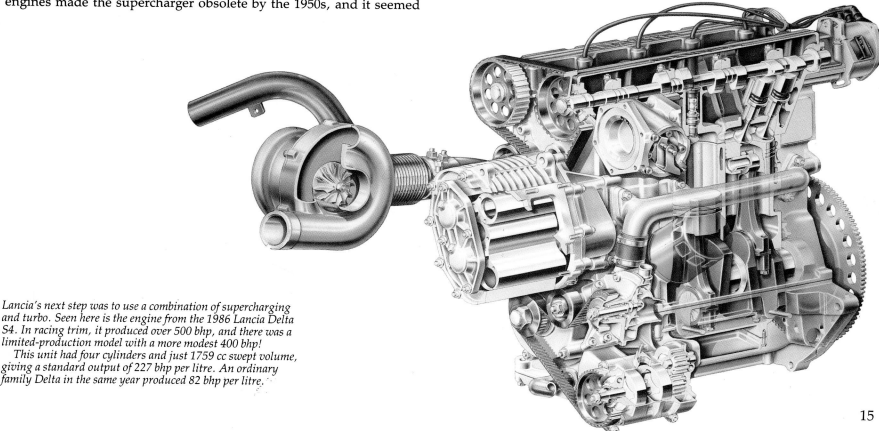

Lancia's next step was to use a combination of supercharging and turbo. Seen here is the engine from the 1986 Lancia Delta S4. In racing trim, it produced over 500 bhp, and there was a limited-production model with a more modest 400 bhp!

This unit had four cylinders and just 1759 cc swept volume, giving a standard output of 227 bhp per litre. An ordinary family Delta in the same year produced 82 bhp per litre.

Among the most advanced vehicles built in the 1970s and 1980s was the Fiat
ECV, equivalent to the Lancia Delta S4. ECV stands for Experimental Composite Vehicle, and was a study by Fiat to show how far the new technology
had come.
   The main structures of the body, instrument panel, even the wheels and
drive shaft, were made of carbon fibre–an extremely strong material that
will probably be common in the future. This Lancia, which never raced, had
a 4-cylinder 1759-cc twin turbo engine giving over 600 bhp.

The engine-driven supercharger made a comeback in the 1980s, being offered by Ford and Volkswagen among the major manufacturers. This TVR 350i (above) has a Sprintex S screw-type supercharger, which sucks in air at about 500 cubic feet per minute at its maximum speed of 15,500 rpm. Giving the 3.5-litre Rover V8 unit an output of 270 bhp, the Sprintex was not a factory option but was fitted by Haughins, the Northern TVR Centre. They also offered a supercharged Range Rover.

Volkswagen G-Lader

Next to try supercharging was Volkswagen who, in 1985, produced a limited run of 500 Polos equipped with the G-Lader compressor, so called because of the G-shaped spirals in the compressor. They were operated by an eccentric shaft which expanded an inner chamber, at the same time compressing the air in an outer chamber, eventually expelling it into the engine. A 1.3-litre Polo so equipped enjoyed an increase in power from 75 to 115 bhp, a little more than the output of a normally-aspirated 1.8-litre Golf engine.

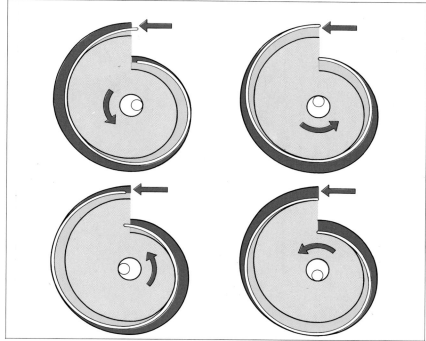

A further batch of 1000 G-Lader-equipped Polos was made in 1987, and a very limited run of of 70 supercharged and four-wheel-drive Golfs in 1989. The G-Lader was offered on a special 4×4 version of the Passat, and was standard on the Corrado sports coupé. KKK, known for their turbochargers, are studying a new kind of supercharger based on the Wankel rotary-engine principle.

In 1985, Volkswagen made a limited run of 500 Polos equipped with the G-Lader compressor (above). In the G supercharger, air is inducted and compressed by two spirals in a G-shaped blower. This blower makes a circular movement in the two-part aluminium housing, thus reducing the compression space and yielding uniform compression of the air towards the centre of the housing, from where the air is forced into the cylinder via an intercooler. The blower is engine-driven by an eccentric auxiliary shaft via a twin V-belt.

Twin cams and multivalve engines

If the designer preferred not to go for turbocharging, the alternative route to greater power lay in increasing the valve area for each cylinder. Four smaller valves will allow a greater area than two larger ones–for it is always possible to cover a given area more completely with a large number of small objects than with a small number of large objects. Another advantage is that the sparking plug can be placed in the ideal position, in the centre of the cylinder.

The four-valve principle was not new, having been tried by Ernest Henry in his remarkable 1912 Grand Prix Peugeots, but it became increasingly fashionable during the 1980s. Most layouts have involved the use of twin overhead camshafts, each pair of valves being operated by one camshaft. But the Triumph Dolomite Sprint engine of 1973 made do with one camshaft, and with no more cams than usual. Each lobe operated an inlet valve directly and an exhaust valve indirectly, through a rocker bearing on the other side of it. Although it worked well it was likely to lead to excessive camshaft wear, and 1980s designs have all involved twin camshafts.

The beginning of the 1980s saw the first multi-valve engines, starting with a few high-performance models, to become standard in most cars at the end of the period. Shown here (right) is the cylinder head of a Volvo 740 16V. Obviously the technique is used because more valves mean better breathing.

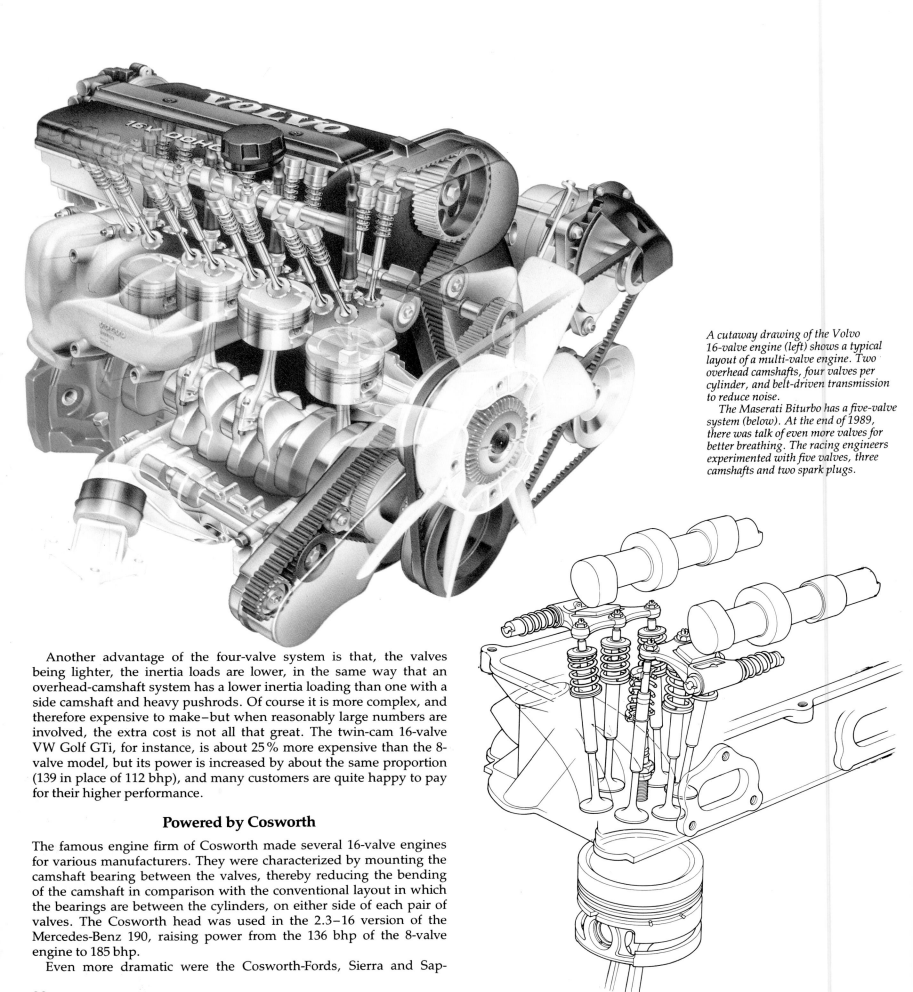

A cutaway drawing of the Volvo 16-valve engine (left) shows a typical layout of a multi-valve engine. Two overhead camshafts, four valves per cylinder, and belt-driven transmission to reduce noise.

The Maserati Biturbo has a five-valve system (below). At the end of 1989, there was talk of even more valves for better breathing. The racing engineers experimented with five valves, three camshafts and two spark plugs.

Another advantage of the four-valve system is that, the valves being lighter, the inertia loads are lower, in the same way that an overhead-camshaft system has a lower inertia loading than one with a side camshaft and heavy pushrods. Of course it is more complex, and therefore expensive to make–but when reasonably large numbers are involved, the extra cost is not all that great. The twin-cam 16-valve VW Golf GTi, for instance, is about 25% more expensive than the 8-valve model, but its power is increased by about the same proportion (139 in place of 112 bhp), and many customers are quite happy to pay for their higher performance.

Powered by Cosworth

The famous engine firm of Cosworth made several 16-valve engines for various manufacturers. They were characterized by mounting the camshaft bearing between the valves, thereby reducing the bending of the camshaft in comparison with the conventional layout in which the bearings are between the cylinders, on either side of each pair of valves. The Cosworth head was used in the 2.3–16 version of the Mercedes-Benz 190, raising power from the 136 bhp of the 8-valve engine to 185 bhp.

Even more dramatic were the Cosworth-Fords, Sierra and Sap-

phire, whose engines were turbocharged as well as having 16 valves. The Sierra was made in three-door form with an enormous 'tea tray' spoiler, from 1986 to 1987, with 204 or 224 bhp from its 1993-cc engine, giving a top speed of 150 mph, or more with various tuning kits. The Sapphire was more civilized, a four-door saloon with less obvious spoiler, but was just as fast. Even though it was expensive compared with other Sapphires, £21,300 when a more basic 2-litre Sapphire cost £10,460, it was good value for money.

Since June 1989 the regular Sierras and Sapphires have also used twin-cam engines, but with only two valves per cylinder. The I4 engine was aimed at economy and low emission levels rather than performance.

Honda takes the lead

Honda began the multi-valve route with a three-valve-per-cylinder (two inlet, one exhaust) engine known as the CVCC (Compound Vortex Controlled Combustion). First seen on the 1972 Civic, it was later made in a variety of sizes from 1232 cc – used in the Jazz – to 1834 cc in the Accord and Prelude. In 1985 they brought out a twin-over-

Providing competition for the more powerful Type 4 cars were these high-performance versions of family saloons, a breed which flourished from the mid-1980s onward. The Peugeot 405 Mi16 and the 16-valve Citroen BX19 GTi were, in a sense, Type 4 cars in reverse. For under their very different bodyshells, they shared the same engines, as did their less powerful sisters.

The Mercedes-Benz 190E 2.3 16V (above) was similar, using the bodyshell of the basic small Mercedes and a Cosworth-designed 16-valve twin-cam engine and Getrag gearbox. The body was subtly modified with front and rear spoilers and side skirts, but all was in the best Stuttgart taste. From 1988 the engine was enlarged to 2.5 litres, giving 185 bhp.

head-camshaft engine with four valves per cylinder, used in the CRX sports coupé and Accord and Integra saloons. Their V6 Legend had a 24-valve engine with one camshaft per bank of cylinders, also used in the Rover 800. Mitsubishi went a step further with their five-valve-per-cylinder 548-cc 3-cylinder unit, for the remarkable Dangan ZZ minicar.

"Select the number of valves with a switch"

The multi-valve layout was not confined to 4 cylinders, of course. Porsche brought out a 32-valve V8 with four camshafts, two to each bank of cylinders, for their 928 S4 of 1986. The ultimate in number of valves in one engine was achieved by Cizeta-Moroder, whose 5995-cc V16 boasted 64 valves.

One of the most interesting engines of the late 1980s was the four-cam 32-valve V8 developed by Lotus for the Chevrolet Corvette ZR1. Capacity was almost the same as the standard Corvette, at 5727 compared with 5733 cc, but the ZR1 gave 385 compared with 245 bhp.

There were two groups of intake ports, valves and cam lobes, and the secondary ports could be deactivated by a so-called 'granny switch', so that only three valves per cylinder were operating. The second inlet valve moved but did not feed any mixture to the cylinder. The switch was operated by a key which the owner could keep, thus restricting the speed when the ZR1 was being driven by less skilled people, such as parking attendants.

Expensive catalytic converters

One of the major preoccupations of the 1970s and 1980s has been the pollution of the atmosphere by car exhausts. It began in California, particularly Los Angeles where the combination of sunshine and

exhausts produced the notorious smog that shut out the sunshine for which the city had been famous, and endangered health to such an extent that in 1988 there were 75 days of smog so bad that children and the elderly were advised to stay indoors. This would indicate that twenty years of anti-pollution regulations had not had much effect, and the city is now considering drastic restrictions on the use of cars.

The initial response to the problem was to equip the exhaust system with a catalytic converter. This was a canister containing platinum, rhodium, palladium and other elements which largely eliminated the harmful hydrocarbons, carbon monoxide and oxides of nitrogen, converting them to water, carbon dioxide and nitrogen.

First introduced in the 1960s, regulations were progressively tightened, so that by 1989 the converter had to eliminate 96% of hydrocarbons and carbon monoxide, and 75% of nitrogen oxides. Unfortunately the catalysts tend to lose their efficiency in service. A report from the American EPA (Environmental Protection Agency) indicated that, after 50,000 miles, some 'cats' might be allowing virtually untreated exhaust gases through. They were thought to reduce performance and tended to increase fuel consumption, although some European tests found this not to be so.

Converters are also expensive to install, adding at least $500 to the average cost of an American car, and they use rare elements. The cost included replacement of the carburetter by a fuel-injection system, necessary for accurate control of the mixture. The fuel-consumption aspect was of particular concern to manufacturers and to the US Government, since conservation of fuel was almost as important to the Administration as cleaning up the atmosphere.

By 1993, manufacturers were expected to build cars averaging at least 39 mpg, compared with the 1989 figure of 33 mpg. This would be impossible with the current design of catalytic converter, so an alternative solution had to be found.

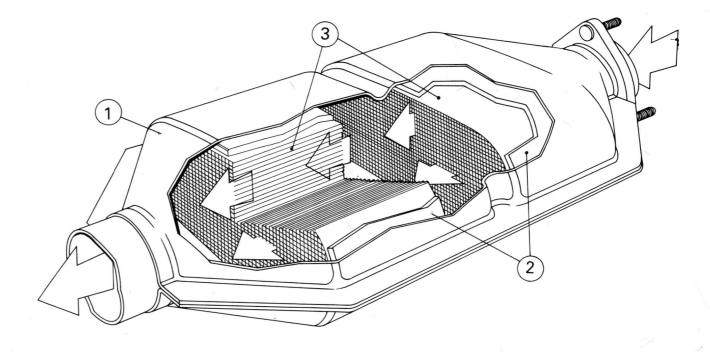

A catalytic converter is a very simple thing with few components. Inside the stainless-steel canister (1) is an elastic retainer (2) made of steel wires, protecting the chemical plates. The cleaning elements (3) are extremely thin ceramic plates covered with platinum and rhodium. When the exhaust gases pass them, most of the harmful elements are eliminated and converted to water, carbon dioxide and nitrogen. However, the conversion process itself is quite complicated and much research is being done on how to improve such devices.

Lean-burn engines

European designers were not at first fond of the 'cat', because of its restriction on performance—which clearly hit smaller engines more severely—and because it was likely to wear out even more quickly under European driving conditions, which involved more use of lower gears, and therefore higher engine speeds.

Rather than burning fuel dirtily (and wastefully) and then cleaning it up afterwards, it seemed more logical to burn it cleanly in the first place. This led to the 'lean-burn' engine, which burns a mixture using less fuel and more air.

For years the average air/fuel ratio has been between 12 and 14:1 parts by weight, although with a partial throttle opening the engine will run satisfactorily at 16:1. At this ratio the carbon monoxide level in the exhaust has dropped very sharply, but the nitrous oxide level is at its highest. The optimum ratio is between 18 and 20:1, as after that the hydrocarbon level starts to rise again, though this may be reduced by further research.

A conventional engine will not function at this optimum ratio, but if a swirl is induced in the mixture just before ignition, it will burn satisfactorily. Research into lean burn has therefore been concentrated on achieving the ideal swirl. Two systems are favoured: axial swirl, which resembles a vertical spring, and transverse or barrel swirl. Swirl is induced during the induction stroke, and maintained during the compression stroke, the upward movement of the piston creating ideal turbulence just before ignition. The swirl is induced by careful shaping of the inlet port and combustion chamber.

Ford was the first manufacturer to introduce the concept of lean burn in production-car engines. That was in 1983, and the range of models available with lean-burn units was still expanding at the end of the 1980s. In the lean-burn cycle (below), incoming gases are forced by the specially designed inlets to swirl rapidly as they enter the combustion chamber.

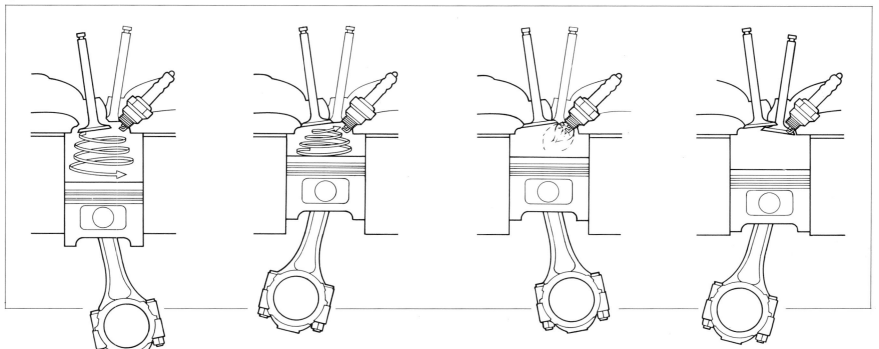

COMBUSTION SYSTEMS ·

```
                    COMBUSTION SYSTEMS

         Inner intermittent              Outer continous

    Homogeneous    Unhomogeneous    Compression        Rankine
                                    ignition           (steam)

  Rotary  Piston engine    Spark ignition      Diesel    Stirling

     2-stroke   4-stroke   Stratified charge  Direct injection  Gas turbine

        Pre-chamber    Direct injection   Multispray   Single/dual
                                                        spray
```

In the last half of the 1980s, car engineers were working hard with various combustion systems—always aiming for lower fuel consumption, while seeking alternative engine concepts and fuel supplies. The companies spent enormous sums of money to meet the future demands for cheaper motoring, but more critical was the growing awareness of air pollution. In this illustration, it is obvious that normal combustion systems predominated—but some examples of experimental engines were built long ago (far left). In fact, the steam engine is older than the car industry, and gas turbines are of the same age as jet planes.

Axial swirl was favoured by Ford and Toyota, barrel swirl by Gaydon Technology who are an experimental arm of the Rover Group. In 1983 Ford introduced their CVH 1.4- and 1.6-litre engine built at Valencia, which had limited swirl achieved by masking an area of the inlet valve. This was called the First Generation lean-burn engine, and was followed by the Second Generation 1.4-litre and V6 engines of 1986, and the Third Generation twin-overhead-camshaft 2-litre I4 engines introduced in 1989 for the Sierra and Scorpio. These ran on a ratio of 19:1.

"I Love Unleaded": the search for alternative fuels

The addition of the organic compound tetraethyl lead, or TEL, to petrol dates back to the 1920s, when it was a useful remedy for knocking and pinking which occurred in the long and shallow combustion chambers of side-valve engines. It continued to be used without arousing any comment until the 1960s, when the growing use of catalytic converters in California, and later elsewhere, made the removal of TEL from petrol a necessity. For a 'cat' will not work long with ordinary fuel, which 'poisons' the elements in it.

Research also indicated that lead damaged plant life, and stunted brain growth in children, although the real extent of this is still controversial. Gradually the use of unleaded fuel spread across the rest of the United States, and in addition the EPA mandated maximum levels of TEL which were permitted in all leaded petrol sold. This began at 0.4 grams per gallon, reducing to 0.2 in December 1986 and to below 0.1 by September 1988.

Leaded fuel was still available, but in diminishing quantities, and some large urban areas were completely without it by 1989. The loss of leaded fuel presented a problem to owners of older cars which could not be easily converted, particularly to high-performance collector cars made between 1950 and the 1980s. These relied on TEL to lubricate the interface between the valves and their seats, and the loss of leaded threatened to greatly reduce valve life.

The solution was to install stellited valve seats and exhaust valves, and there were a number of additives available. These were mostly liquid, but there was also Carbonflo, a 22-mm cartridge containing a tin-based compound which could be inserted in the fuel tank. It was claimed to improve running and fuel consumption, as well as enabling any engine to run satisfactorily on unleaded petrol. Initial fears about loss of performance with unleaded fuel were not substantiated. Tests of a Ford Sierra XR4×4 showed a reduction of top speed from 124.5 to 124.0 mph, and in 0–60 mph from 9.6 to 9.7 seconds, while acceleration in top gear was, at some speeds, better with unleaded fuel.

Forest death calls for unleaded fuel

The first controls on exhaust emissions and testing in Europe came in 1971, but not until the mid-1980s did really strict and widespread regulations come into effect. These reduced the acceptable level of hydrocarbon and nitrogen oxides by nearly a third below previous levels, and carbon monoxide by 40%. This could only be achieved by catalytic converters, which necessitated unleaded petrol.

Germany, acutely aware of pollution problems because of its dying forests, led the way. By 1988, unleaded petrol accounted for 52.7% of total sales in West Germany, and was available at 75% of its filling stations. Denmark was even further ahead with 90%, and in Holland every petrol outlet sold unleaded. Britain was slower to follow, with the first all-unleaded garage not coming into operation until January 1989. However, it was expected that by the end of 1989, unleaded petrol would account for 20% of all sales. Not everyone loved the stuff: early in 1989, Italy's sales were 1.3%, France's less than 1%, and in Spain it was not available at all.

Many European countries introduced tax concessions on unleaded fuel, and Germany also offered concessions on the purchase of cars fitted with catalytic converters. As a result, in 1988 only 3% of German car buyers chose non-catalyst petrol cars. EEC regulations stated that by October 1990 all new cars must be able to run on unleaded fuel, by January 1992 all new cars over 2 litres must be fitted with catalytic converters, and by January 1993 this would be extended to all new cars of any size. In 1989 Skoda became the first manufacturer from the Eastern Bloc to offer a catalytic converter, on their Favorit.

Diesel engines

The widespread use of unleaded fuel and catalytic converters in so-called 'green cars' led many optimists to believe that the threat to the atmosphere had been lifted. Unfortunately this was not the case. Granted, there was less lead to damage children's brains, and fewer hydrocarbons to cause tree-killing acid rain. But the 'cat' converted carbon monoxide to carbon dioxide, which is one of the main causes

Diesel engines were, for numerous reasons, not very popular during the 1950s and 1960s. In spite of cheap fuel and immense distances driven between overhauls, diesel engines were noisy and nasty-smelling, as well as less powerful than their petrol-feed relatives. They were also expensive to build and maintain. These virtues commended them to commercial use, as in taxis and long-distance haulage. Yet in the 1980s, the situation changed completely and almost all manufacturers had a diesel model for sale.

The diesel engine works on the same principles as the four-stroke engine: induction, compression, expansion and exhaust. The main difference is that the diesel's fuel is not supplied until air is fully compressed in the cylinder. The compression is much higher than normal, at 22–24:1 compared with 8–9:1 for a petrol engine. This makes the air so hot that the fuel self-ignites when sprayed into the combustion chambers. Therefore a diesel engine has no ignition system, only a glow plug for cold-starting.

The engine shown here is a Volvo TD24 from the late 1980s, used in the 700 series.

of the Greenhouse Effect, the gradual heating-up of the atmosphere that will lead, among other things, to the melting of polar ice caps.

The lean-burn engine was less damaging in this respect–but even better, and more widespread, was the diesel engine. Diesels had been popular in heavy commercial vehicles for more than fifty years. In 1931, *The Autocar* said: 'The oil engine has come to stay for use in heavy motors and aeroplanes; will it reach the private car world?'

The first diesel car was offered, by Mercedes-Benz, in 1936. Fiat joined them in the 1950s. Drawbacks were the need for powerful batteries to turn a cold diesel engine over, the vibration, noise and offensive exhaust fumes. But by the late 1970s, diesels were part of the range of many European manufacturers, as well as gaining a sudden and perhaps unexpected acceptance in America–unexpected because America had always been the land of the large, gas-guzzling petrol engine. Even on heavy trucks, Americans were much later to turn to diesels than the Europeans. Yet the fuel crisis concentrated the American mind on economy, and the diesel engine was one of the answers.

Unpopular in America . . .

General Motors was the leading firm to offer diesels, which they did from 1978, initially on the 5.7-litre V8 used in the Oldsmobile Delta and 98. Although diesels of V6 and V8 configuration were subsequently used in some models of Buick, Cadillac, Chevrolet and Pontiac as well, all GM diesel engines were made in Oldsmobile's Lansing factory.

Until very recently the appeal of the diesel was economic, not environmental. And when the threat of fuel shortages began to recede in the mid-1980s, America turned sharply away from diesels. Lower specific output and noisy running were the main objections. For example, a 1984 Chevrolet Celebrity with 4293-cc V6 diesel engine developed only 85 bhp, compared with 110 bhp from the 3785-cc petrol unit.

GM dropped their diesels after 1985, and the only other manufacturer to make any was Ford, who offered a diesel option in the Escort and Mercury Lynx from 1984 to 1987, and a turbodiesel option in the 1984–5 Lincolns. In 1989, the only diesels on the US market were the VW Jetta, reintroduced after a two-year absence, and the Mercedes-Benz 190.

. . . but just the opposite in Europe

European diesels were much more widespread, being offered in the hatchback ranges of Citroen, Fiat, Ford, Opel, Peugeot, Renault, Seat, Vauxhall and Volkswagen, as well as in larger cars such as the Austin Montego, Citroen BX, CX and XM, Fiat Croma, Mercedes-Benz 190, 200 and 250, Opel Vectra, Peugeot 305, 309, 405 and 505, Renault 9, 11, 19, 21 and 25, Range Rover, Volkswagen Passat and Volvo 240 and 760.

Many of the higher-performance models used turbochargers to boost the somewhat lethargic output of a normally aspirated diesel. A turbocharged, intercooled, three-valve-per-cylinder, 2.1-litre Citroen XM was comparable in performance to a 2-litre catalyst-equipped petrol version. In fact it was one mph faster in top speed, while its fuel consumption, at 44 mpg, was almost 12 mpg better than its petrol rival.

Most diesels had indirect fuel injection, where the mixture is sprayed into a small pre-combustion chamber inside the cylinder head, connected by a narrow passage to one side of the actual head. The fuel ignites in the pre-chamber, expanding the partly burning fuel-air mixture so that it is forced out of the passage into the main space above the piston.

In 1988 Fiat, closely followed by Austin-Rover, developed a direct-injection engine which dispenses with the pre-combustion chamber. This is simpler but requires a lot of swirl if the mixture is to be blended properly, so the cylinder head design is very important. The fuel is burnt more efficiently, and there is no heat loss in travelling down to passage for the pre-chamber. Thus, fuel consumption is better than in an indirect-injection diesel: about 40% better than an equivalent-size petrol engine compared with 25% improvement from an indirect-injection unit. Servicing intervals are also longer–about double the 4,500 miles of an indirect-injection engine, which suffers from carbon contamination of the oil.

Dramatic growth

European sales of diesel-engined cars have grown dramatically since 1970, when they represented less than 10% of the total, and only Mercedes-Benz, Peugeot and the Belgian-marketed Volga were in the market. In the EEC alone, 1,066,820 were sold by 1982, and five years later the figure had risen to about 1.8 million. Germany was the leader among Friends of the Diesel, with Italy very close behind. This is perhaps surprising in view of Italy's lack of interest in unleaded petrol, but until very recently the appeal of diesels has been solely on grounds of economy. Now that it has been found environmentally friendly as well, sales should rise still further.

The only cloud on the horizon is the accusation that the carbon particulants (soot) emitted by the diesel might be a cause of cancer. This caused a drop in German diesel sales for 1988, but direct injection and catalytic converters modified for diesel application were probable answers to the problem. VW's Unwalt diesel shown at the 1989 Frankfurt Show had an oxidation converter said to absorb up to 50% of the aromatic hydrocarbons. At the same show Audi offered a direct-injection turbo diesel of 2+ litres, which was to be used in the 100TDi saloons and Avant estates from January 1990.

Methanol and alcohol

Two other fuels which were gaining popularity in the period were methanol and alcohol. The former is a high-octane fuel, produced from coal or natural gas, which has been used as an additive to racing fuels for decades. It produces little in the way of hydrocarbons or nitrous oxides, so it is not a smog creator. But its output of carbon dioxide is twice that of petrol, so it is bad for the Greenhouse Effect.

Nevertheless, it has found favour in southern California, where by 1993 all fleet vehicles, including buses and hire-cars, will have to run on methanol. By 2007 there will be a complete ban on petrol and diesel engines in the area, if the proposed legislation goes ahead according to plan. Already Ford and General Motors offer engines adapted to run on methanol as well as petrol, or a mixture of the two. By 1993 they expected to make at least 100,000 variable-fuel cars per year. Two fuel companies, Arco and Chevron, planned to offer methanol from many of their outlets by 1990.

Alcohol fuel has been largely confined to Brazil, but it is well established there, with about 40% of the country's 11.5 million vehicles using it. Produced from sugar cane and sold by farmers' distilleries to the national company, Petrobras, alcohol fuel was kept at 55% of the price of petrol–in order to encourage production of a local asset, and to increase sales of cars whose owners might be deterred by the higher cost of petrol. Consumption of alcohol was 33% higher than petrol and performance inferior.

Transmissions

The most important development in drive systems over the past two decades has undoubtedly been that of four-wheel drive. In 1970 it was confined to more or less utilitarian vehicles such as the Jeeps and Toyota Land Cruiser. Even the excellent and comfortable Range Rover was not an ordinary saloon. The only exception was the remarkable Jensen FF, a four-wheel-drive version of the Interceptor GT coupé. This used the Ferguson System with a master differential and two one-way clutches, providing permanent four-wheel drive and a front/rear power split of 37/63.

According to Tony Sheldon, chairman of Harry Ferguson Research, this was about the same ratio as on a dog or horse. The FF also featured Dunlop Maxaret anti-lock brakes, the only car to have this system. It was a magnificent high-speed tourer, setting new standards of traction and road holding, but suffered from teething troubles and also from its high price. The ordinary Interceptor was not cheap, at £5,838 in 1970, but an FF cost £7,705. In appearance they were almost identical, though the FF was four inches longer and could be quickly identified by the twin cooling slots behind the front wheel arches. Only 387 FFs were made, compared with 5,577 Interceptors.

The Jensen FF (Ferguson Formula) was a supercar long before its time. A four-wheel-drive version of the Interceptor GT coupé, it used the Ferguson system with master differential and two one-way clutches. But it brought Jensen to the brink of ruin and, to cover the losses, the company had to sell four Interceptors for every FF.

An important feature of the Ferguson system was the viscous coupling (VC) which limited the slip in the central differential. This involved two sets of closely spaced and interleaved circular discs, immersed in a highly viscous silicone-based fluid. Its viscosity was such that at low speeds the resistance was small, enabling one set of discs to revolve rather easily relative to the others, but at higher speeds the fluid friction rose very sharply, effectively locking the discs together.

This limits the slip induced by wheelspin, yet it is wear-free compared with a mechanical limited-slip differential. After the Jensen FF was dropped in 1971, no further applications of the viscous coupling

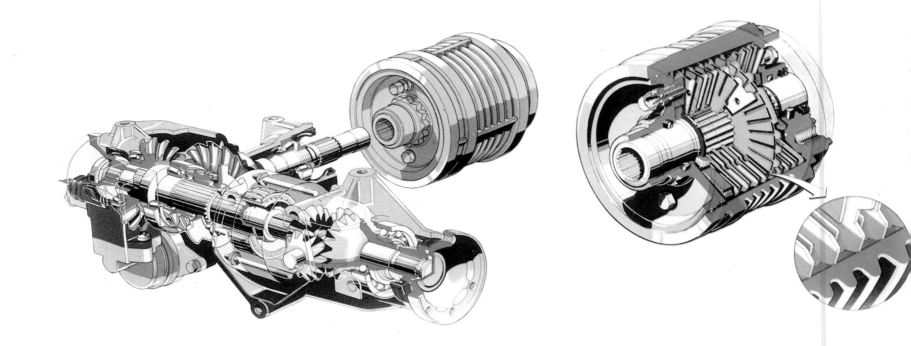

were seen until 1980, when it was taken up by American Motors for their new range of Eagle 4×4 sedans, coupés and station wagons. Their transmissions were made under Ferguson licence by the New Process Gear Company, a division of Chrysler.

Four-wheel drive: ever more popular

The 1980s have seen a great increase in the numbers of 4×4 passenger cars, many of which have used the viscous coupling. These included the Ford Sierra XR4×4 and Scorpio, the BMW 325iX, Lancia Prisma and Delta, Nissan Pulsar, and Volkswagen Synchro Golf and Transporter. Introduced in 1986, the VWs had a variable distribution of power between front and rear wheels, according to the steepness or surface of the road. The ratio varied between 90/10 for normal conditions and 0/100 for exceptionally steep and slippery hills.

The cutaway drawing of a viscous coupling (left) shows the rear-axle drive, together with the differential, freewheel and viscous coupling itself. The container (above) holds a clutch housing, whose inner and outer clutch plates are connected respectively with the prop shaft and rear-axle gears. The container is filled with a viscous silicon fluid, changes its viscosity according to the axle speed, and thus serves as a power transmission between the clutch plates.

This was effected by having the front wheels permanently driven as in the front-wheel-drive Golf, and the rear wheels driven through a viscous coupling only. Thus when the front wheels lose adhesion, the coupling tightens up and transfers some power to the rear wheels. Ford has produced some variations on the VC theme: the Escort Turbo RS used it on the front wheels only, while the RS200 mid-engined rally car had three VCs, one in each axle differential as well

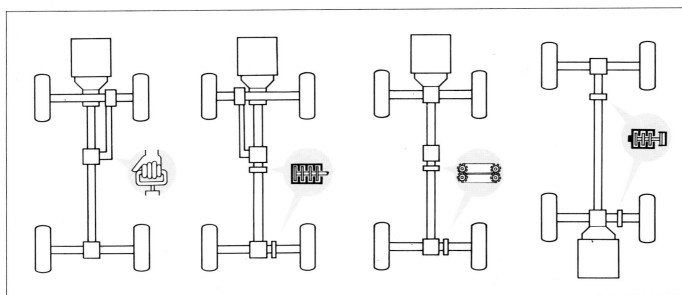

MITSUBISHI SHOGUN

Four-wheel drive:	Part-time
Central drive device:	Transfer box
Central drive lock:	Rigid 4wd
Front/rear torque split:	Variable
Rear differential lock:	Optional lsd

FORD SIERRA XR 4×4

Four-wheel drive:	Permanent
Central drive device:	Epicyclic diff
Central drive lock:	Viscous coupling
Front/rear torque split:	34/66
Rear differential lock:	Viscous coupling

AUDI V8 (MANUAL)

Four-wheel drive:	Permanent
Central drive device:	Torsen diff
Central drive lock:	Torsen diff
Front/rear torque split:	50/50
Rear differential lock:	Torsen diff

PORSCHE 959

Four-wheel drive:	Permanent
Central drive device:	Hydraulic clutch
Central drive lock:	Hydraulic clutch
Front/rear torque split:	Variable
Rear differential lock:	Hydraulic clutch

Ford's RS200 4×4 was built with Group B rallying in mind–though it never reached its full potential in this field, as Group B was cancelled at the end of its first season in 1986. Power was transmitted from the 1.8-litre Ford Cosworth BDA engine via a five-speed gearbox and three viscous couplings: one in each axle differential and a centrally mounted one. Exactly 200 were made, all finished in white, and built for Ford by Reliant.

The top model in the Delta range was the HF Turbo 4WD. It was not only a rally winner, but also a very impressive road car, for both summer and winter conditions. The four-wheel-drive system had Ferguson viscous coupling as well as a Torsen differential. Standard output was 200 bhp, but the rally cars produced 295 bhp at 7,000 rpm.

as one in the central differential. The torque split could be varied by the driver, from 37/63 on good roads to around 50/50 when greater traction was needed.

Another successful rally car using viscous coupling for its 4×4 drive was the Peugeot 205T16. Campaigned from 1984–85, when they won nine out of twelve Championship rallies, the Peugeots had mid-mounted engines and elliptical mid-mounted transfer boxes which distributed power 34/66. Another company to use VC was Subaru, who introduced it on the 544-cc Rex microcar in 1987. This had no conventional rear differential, but instead a Twin Visco coupling, which acted as a central and rear differential combined.

Not all designers of four-wheel-drive systems favoured VC. Subaru introduced their 4×4 saloons, estates and pick-ups in 1974, using full-time drive to the front wheels with a selectable four-wheel drive from a central differential to the rear wheels. Although less sophisticated than the later cars using VC, the Subarus were pioneers in reasonably priced 4×4 vehicles, and introduced many people to the benefits of four-wheel drive.

The next most significant car was the Audi Quattro of 1980, which featured permanent four-wheel drive from a bevel-gear central differential that gave a 50/50 distribution of power. It was a simple system, but had a drawback: if either or both wheels on one axle started to

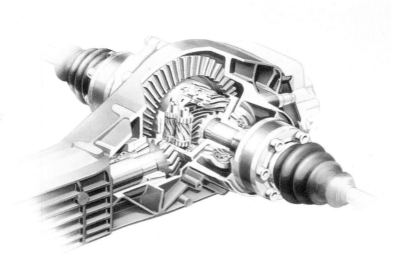

tion through its worm to its worm-wheel. That worm-wheel is geared to the other, though, which cannot drive its mating worm, so the system locks up, and all the available power is transferred immediately to the wheels with the most grip.

When *Motor* Magazine tested two Quattro 80 saloons, one with a normal differential and the other with the Torsen, they found that the former suffered considerable wheelspin when the clutch was engaged at 4,000 rpm on a wet surface, the latter none at all. Following the success of the original Quattro coupé, Audi extended four-wheel drive through their range—to the 80, 90, 100 and 200 saloons, the V8 saloon and the new coupé Quattro, not to be confused with the original Quattro which remained in production until the end of the 1980s.

spin on a slippery surface, the differential directed all the power to the spinning wheels, just the opposite of what was needed.

The Torsen differential

The second-generation Quattros made from 1984 onwards had a central Torsen limited-slip differential. This system, which derives its name from the words TORque and SENsing, uses the principle that a worm-and-wheel gearing is increasingly irreversible when the worm's grooves approach a right-angle setting to its longitudinal axis. The worm can drive the wheel but not vice versa. Thus when one pair of wheels loses adhesion, the drive shaft at the low-grip end of the car tries to rotate as the wheels start to spin, and can transmit that rota-

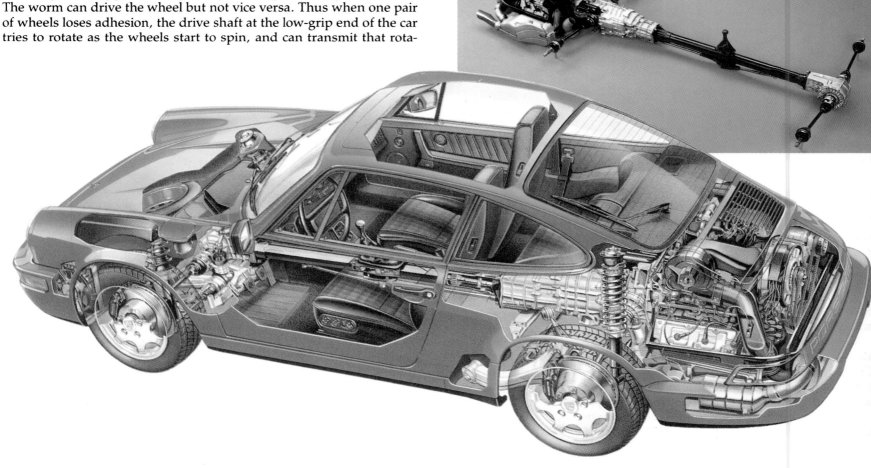

Two of the many cars endowed with four-wheel drive in the 1980s. The Fiat Panda (right), made in 4×4 form since 1983, had the larger Panda engine of 999 cc and a transmission developed for Fiat by Steyr-Puch. It was the cheapest 4×4 on the market, though closely rivalled by the Lada Niva and the Subaru Justy, which had a 1.2-litre 3-cylinder engine and, like the Panda, optional four-wheel drive.

In 1980 American Motors launched their new range of Eagle 4×4 sedans, coupés and station wagons with the viscous-coupling limited-slip central differential, also used in the Ferguson-equipped Jensen FF 4×4. Shown here (below right) is a 1984 Eagle wagon. Although the Eagles had off-road ability, the company promoted them more as ultra-safe vehicles for road use, particularly in snow. They were made until 1987, many more wagons than sedans being built.

The 4×4 principle soon spread across a wide spectrum of cars: from the Fiat Panda, cheapest of the 4×4s and the first transverse-engined car to drive on all wheels, through the rally-winning Lancia Delta and Mazda 323, to the highly sophisticated Mitsubishi Galant with four-wheel steering as well as four-wheel drive. In 1988, the first 4×4 people-carriers appeared in the new Nissan Prairie and Renault Espace, while popular family saloons such as the Opel Vectra/Vauxhall Cavalier, Citroen BX and Renault 21, Toyota Camry and VW Jetta were available with viscous coupling four-wheel drive. Porsche used an epicyclic central differential with a 31/69 split on their Carrera 4 of 1988. In the USA, Pontiac offered their 6000 sedan with four-wheel drive from 1989 at $22,599, a hefty $7,200 more than the regular 6000 with front drive only.

Considerable progress was made with automatic transmissions. The unloved two-speeders of the 1960s had given way to three-speeders by the early 1970s even on cheap American cars, while the smaller engines of European and Japanese cars made three speeds mandatory anyway. Minis were still offered with automatics, and anything above that was almost always offered with an automatic option. Exceptions were some Eastern European cars such as Skoda, Wartburg and Yugo. Even Skoda's new front-drive Favorit was without an automatic option, though the manual box did have five speeds.

The supercar owner still expected to change his gears himself—so all cars were manual in the Ferrari Testarossa, Lamborghini and Cizeta category. However, Ferrari surprised customers by offering a three-speed Hydramatic box on the front-engined 400 saloon of 1976, and this was continued on its successor, the 412.

Four-speed automatics were offered by Jaguar on the 1986 XJ6, and in 1989 Nissan became the first manufactuerer to offer a five-speeder—on the Cedric and Gloria, large sedans mainly for the home market.

The extra speed was obtained by two planetary gear sets at the back of the gearbox. An additional feature of the Nissan 5E-AT box was automatic reprogramming, to compensate for changes in clutch engagement timing caused by wear and age.

Chevrolet's Corvette ZR1 had a six-speed with automatic selection of first to fourth when 75% of the power was being used. Above this, the CAGS (Computer Aided Gear Selection) was cancelled so that the driver could enjoy the best of all worlds—automatic for traffic conditions and manual for fast open-road driving. Porsche offered something similar on the 1989 Carrera, but here the change from automatic to manual or vice versa was made by moving the gear lever sideways from one selector channel to another.

This advanced six-speed gearbox was used in Chevrolet's limited-production Corvette ZR1, which offered automatic shifting from first to fourth speeds when up to 75 % of the engine power was being exploited. In the two highest speeds, or under really hard acceleration, this computer-aided gear selection did not operate. So the driver could "have his cake and eat it"—with automatic for traffic, and manual for fast open-road driving.

CVT and CVS: variations on a theme by DAF

A completely different kind of automatic transmission was the continuously variable system known as CVT (by Fiat) or CVS (by Ford). Devised by the Dutch Van Doorne company, makers of DAF cars and trucks, it was originally used on the small DAF cars made from 1958 to 1975, incorporating rubber belts and expanding pulleys which gave different ratios. Known as the Variomatic, its advantage over conventional automatics using planetary gears was that it was infinitely variable, rather than limited to two or three ratios. But the friction losses were considerable with the flexing of the rubber belts, so that it was no more efficient than a planetary system, and was unsuitable to engines of much power. It was used on the DAF-built Volvo 343 until 1982, then dropped in favour of a conventional manual box.

However, Van Doorne continued working on the principle, and in 1987 came up with a greatly improved version, in which the rubber belts were replaced by steel ones working in V-shaped grooves, each formed from a sliding sheave which could be moved relative to a fixed sheave. When the two sheaves are moved together, the vee-belt running between them is forced to ride up to a larger diameter, and when they are separated the belt settles to a smaller diameter.

Thus changes in ratio are achieved by increasing the effective diameter of one pulley and reducing the diameter of the other by a similar amount. The belt itself is inextensible and transmits power in compression, rather than in tension as in the Variomatic and other belt-drive systems.

The steel belts, composed of 300 trapezoidal plates strung together on two layered bands, were made only by Van Doorne. At first they assembled the complete transmission as well, but from 1989 Ford made these in a new £75-million plant at Bordeaux, for use by both themselves and Fiat. Originally available in the 1.1- and 1.4-litre Fiestas and Fiats Uno and Tipo, the system was extended to the 1.6-litre Escort and Orion for 1990, and was used by Subaru in the Justy 4×4 saloon. The Japanese firm assembled its own CVT transmissions, but used Van Doorne-made belts.

In the world of manual gearboxes, all-synchromesh gears had become universal, even on such primitives as the Wartburg. During the 1980s, five forward speeds became increasingly common on small

Simple and ingenious! That mean old belt is replaced by a much stronger modern one. Actually a steel band, this is manufactured by Van Doorne in Holland—father of the Variomatic system and the famous DAF Daffodil car. The material used is Margarin steel, a new spinoff from the space industry. The belt consists of 300 trapezoidal plates, joined on two layered bands made of another type of special steel. A protruding boss and matching recess in each plate limits the relative movement, and hence the friction.

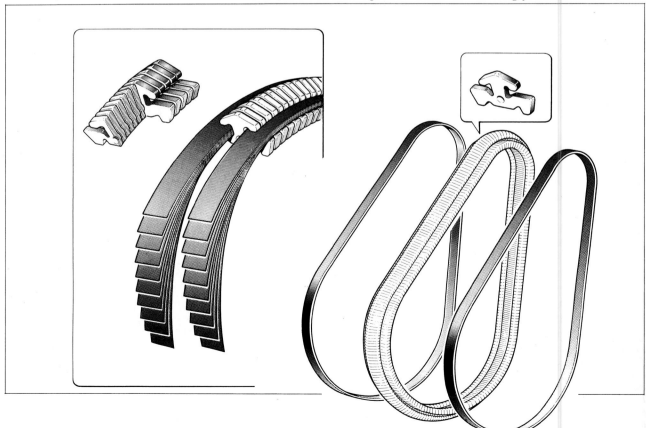

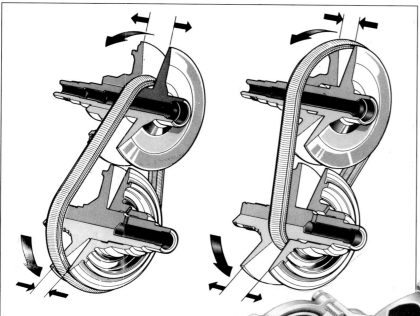

cars, so that Austin's Mini and Metro seemed quite out of step in having only four. Porsche offered six speeds on the limited-production 959, as did BMW on the 850i coupé.

Four-wheel steering

There were few developments in the world of steering until the late 1980s, apart from the increasing adoption of the more precise rack-and-pinion system, and of power assistance. Rolls-Royce's Silver Shadow 1, which used recirculating ball steering, was criticized for its lack of feel ('like driving a rice pudding', one owner said), but things were put right when rack-and-pinion was adopted on the Mark II Shadow of 1977. The Rolls, like all the larger American cars and their European rivals from Jaguar, BMW and Mercedes-Benz, featured power-assisted steering. This spread down the scale, featuring on the top-specification models of such cars as the Peugeot 205 automatic and VW Golf.

(Above) The basic principle is that, by moving the sheaves of two pulleys closer together or farther apart, their effective diameters can be altered to create a wide range of power ratios. The system shown here is used in the Fiat Uno Selecta, where the ratio ranged between 2.47:1 in low gear to 0.445 in high gear.

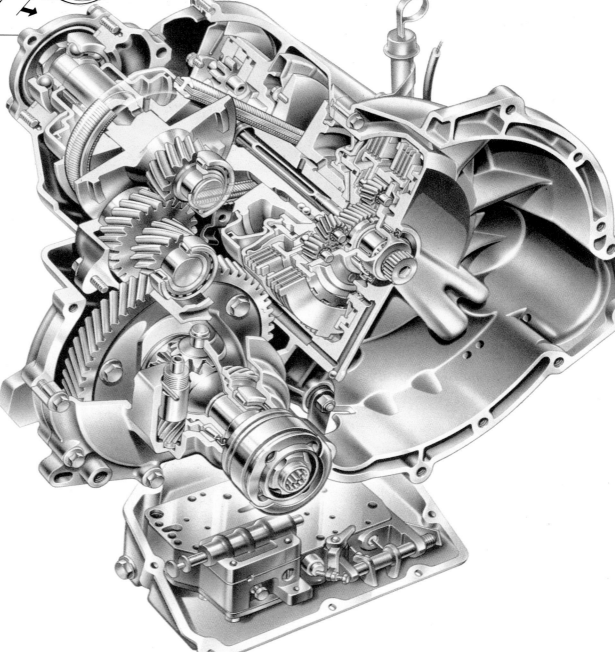

Not only Fiat but also Ford (right) had an automatic transmission, called CTX–Continuously Variable Transaxle. It was virtually identical to the Fiat version. Being much lighter than a conventional automatic transmission, it had a fuel consumption on the same level as a traditional gearbox. One should remember that an argument against automatic gearboxes was always their higher fuel consumption.

33

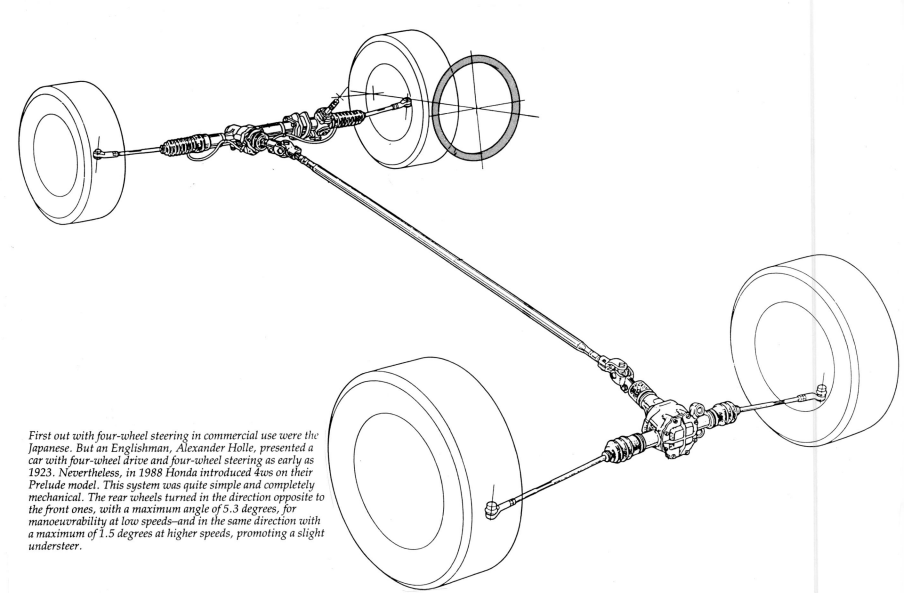

First out with four-wheel steering in commercial use were the Japanese. But an Englishman, Alexander Holle, presented a car with four-wheel drive and four-wheel steering as early as 1923. Nevertheless, in 1988 Honda introduced 4ws on their Prelude model. This system was quite simple and completely mechanical. The rear wheels turned in the direction opposite to the front ones, with a maximum angle of 5.3 degrees, for manoeuvrability at low speeds—and in the same direction with a maximum of 1.5 degrees at higher speeds, promoting a slight understeer.

The Japanese were particularly given to power assistance, offering it on cars as small as the 1.4-litre Honda Civic, and on all Nissans from the Bluebird upwards and Toyotas from the Carina upwards. The Honda Ballade had PAS, yet its British version, the Rover 200 series which could have benefitted just as much from power assistance, never had PAS.

Honda's 4WS system

By far the most important development of the 1980s in steering was its extension to all four wheels. Like so many ideas, this was by no means new, and had been seen as early as 1904 on the electric trucks made by the Couple Gear Co. of Grand Rapids, Michigan. The Jeffery Quad trucks of World War I had four-wheel drive and steering, as did the Latil road and forestry tractors of the 1930s.

A few cars were fitted with the system experimentally, but it was not seen on a production car until 1988. This was the Honda Prelude coupé, whose rear wheels turned initially in the same direction as the front wheels, reaching a maximum of 1.5 degrees of steer for a steering-wheel angle of 127 degrees. Further movement of the steering wheel turned them back to the straight-ahead position at a steering-wheel angle of 232 degrees, which represented nearly three quarters of a turn. Further movement of the wheel up to full lock at 450 degrees turned the rear wheels in the opposite direction to those at the front, to an angle of 5.3 degrees. Opposite-direction steering gave improved manoeuvrability with a reduction in turning circle from

10.6 to 9.6 metres. The same-direction steering, which operated at small turns of the steering wheel, improved high-speed stability by promoting slight understeer.

It was generally thought by testers that there were definite advantages at low speeds, but that the high-speed benefits were very slight, and might be obtained more cheaply by improvements to tyres and suspension.

Mitsubishi offers four-wheel steering and four-wheel drive

The movement of the Honda's rear wheels was achieved mechanically, by a shaft from the front steering rack coupled to a rear-mounted epicyclic steering box. The next 4WS car to appear, Mazda's 626, was the first family saloon to steer on all four wheels, and used a more sophisticated hydraulic rack to move the rear wheels. Like Honda, its wheels steered in opposite directions at low speeds, and in the same direction above 22 mph. The third contender in the field was Mitsubishi, whose Galant Dynamic Four offered a plethora of fashionable features: four-wheel drive, four-wheel steering, self-aligning suspension and anti-lock brakes, as well as the 16-valve engine of the regular Galant.

Like the Mazda, the Galant used a hydraulic control for the rear-wheel steering, but this operated only in the same direction as the front wheels, and only came into operation above 30 mph. Mitsubishi's engineers were unimpressed with the low-speed opposite-

The possibility of simpler, more flexible low-speed manoeuvring was undeniably one of the more pleasant arguments for four-wheel steering. Here are two examples (below left), with Mazda's four-wheel steering (A) and their two-wheel-steered model (B).

In this illustration of reduced turning radius (below right), both cars have the same wheel-base, but the four-wheel-steered car (A) has a considerably smaller turning circle than the two-wheel-steered car (B). Access to narrow spaces is also much easier with four-wheel steering.

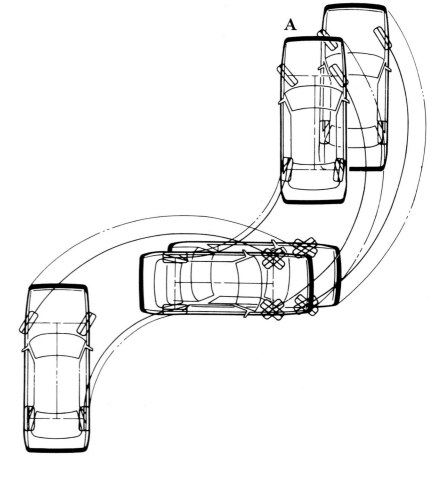

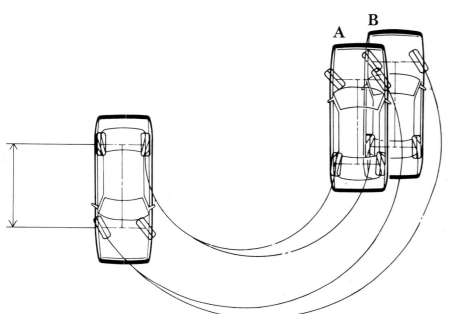

Mitsubishi engineers shunned the technique of opposite steering at low speeds. Their Galant 4wd + 4ws had hydraulically controlled rear-wheel steering, which only came into effect at speeds above 30 mph.

The production saloon is illustrated here by the successful rally car (left), examples of which finished 1st and 5th in the 1989 RAC Rally.

The 4ws system in a Mazda 626 (right) includes power steering at both front and rear: (A) oil pump, (B) front power steering, (C) speed censors, (D) control unit, (E) rear steering shaft, (F) rear power steering, (G) steering wheel.

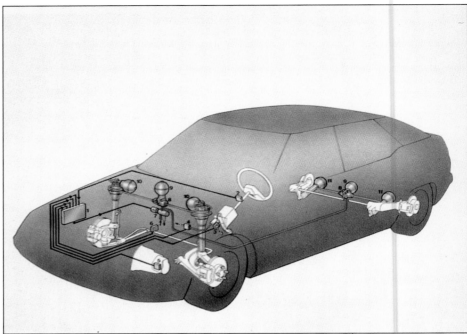

In 1989 the Citroen XM replaced the CX model, and the famous hydropneumatic suspension system took a step further. Above is a schematic illustration of the Hydractive system, whose function is simple. Five sensors register all activity in the steering, brakes, anti-roll bars and accelerator. The sensors tell the system whether the suspension should be soft or hard. When it is soft, all six oleo-pneumatic spheres operate with more gas. If the damping is to be hard, connections to the two centrally located gas chambers are closed.

The front suspension (above right) has three gas chambers. Note the connection between the suspension struts and the anti-roll bar.

direction steering, claiming that it made drivers nervous. The most sophisticated system of all was the HICAS (high-capacity actively controlled suspension) on the 1989 Nissan 300ZX Turbo coupé, which deliberately induced some yaw (rotation of the car about a vertical axis) whereas others tried to kill it. There was a 50-millisecond delay between operation of the steering wheel and the rear wheels, followed by a transient flick of opposite steering before stability-promoting parallel steering took over.

Suspension and braking

By 1970 independent suspension of the front wheels was taken for granted on all passenger vehicles, with the exception of some off-roaders such as the Jeep, Land Rover and Toyota Land Cruiser. Coil-and-wishbone was the most popular technique here, particularly in America where it was usually combined with the old-fashioned semi-elliptic leaf springs at the rear. A variation on this was the McPherson strut, in which the coil was combined with a shock absorber in a vertical strut on a rigid stub axle.

Named after its inventor, the Ford engineer Earle McPherson, it

was first seen on French Fords in 1948, being taken up by the British Ford Consul and Zephyr in 1950, and by the German Fords for 1952. Lotus used McPherson struts at the rear of the 1957 Elite, but it was not until the 1970s that they became really widespread on a great variety of cars.

Although there were many different suspension systems in use during the 1970s, most of them had been developed earlier–such as British Leyland's Hydrolastic interconnected front and rear springs, Citroen's interconnected coils as pioneered on the 2CV in 1948, and the much more sophisticated hydropneumatic system of Citroen's DS series.

Citroen used four oleo-pneumatic sphere-capped struts with gas in compression replacing metal springs, controlled by brake fluid metered by a pump-driven regulator powered by the engine. This adjusted the height of the car from the ground, so that if the regulator was set to high, switching on the engine resulted in the car raising itself by several inches within a few seconds. A development of the 1950s, it was still seen on the DS made until 1975, on its successor the CX, on the smaller GS saloons and the SM coupé.

The year 1989 saw the CX replaced by the XM, which took the hydropneumatic system a step further. Known as Hydractive, and only available on the higher-specification XMs, this added an extra oleo-pneumatic sphere mid-way between the existing ones at both front and rear. This gave variable spring settings: at 'soft', oil flowed from each main sphere into the third sphere, providing a softer spring rate, and softer damping as well. The oil could also flow from one side to the other when the car rolled, reducing roll stiffness.

When the setting was on 'firm', a solenoid fed hydraulic pressure to the third spheres, cutting off oil flow and isolating them from the system, so that each wheel's movement acted against its own sphere only, giving a stiffer rate and firmer damping. With the system on 'firm', spring rates rose by 90% at the front and 80% at the rear, damping by 30 and 50%, and roll stiffness by 15 and 30%. Variation between soft and firm modes was entirely automatic, controlled by a computer which received information from sensors in the steering, braking and suspension system, and acting in a fraction of a second.

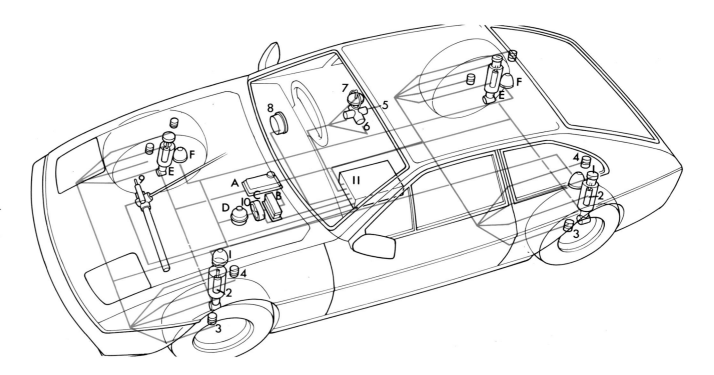

Lotus was the leading company when active suspension systems were developed in the late 1980s. First used in their Formula 1 racing cars, the idea was later taken up by several companies.

In the very complex active-ride system (below), a central control unit has general authority over the four-wheel servos.

Electronics:
1 Load cell, 2 Displacement sensor, 3 Hub accelerometer, 4 Body sprung mass accelerometer, 5 Longitudinal accelerometer, 6 Lateral accelerometer, 7 Yaw rate gyro, 8 Car speed indicator, 9 Steering angle sensor, 10 Hydraulic pressure, 11 Computer.

Hydraulics:
A Reservoir, B Cooler, C Pump, D Filter, E Actuators, F Accumulators.

Active suspension by Lotus

The reaction to information fed from road conditions was taken further in the Active Suspension developed by Lotus in 1987 for their Formula 1 racing cars, and adopted on road cars by Nissan, Toyota, Chevrolet and Mercedes-Benz in 1990. Instead of the usual springs and dampers, this 'active ride' had quick-acting hydraulic struts controlled by sophisticated servo mechanisms, which moved the wheels up and down to conform with the irregularities of the road. These mechanisms were governed by a central computer which received and transmitted information in milliseconds.

The system could completely eliminate roll of body and wheels– the bane of fast cornering, as it reduced the area of tyre acting on the road. Originally the servo mechanisms replaced conventional suspensions, but Lotus soon added ordinary coil springs in parallel with the hydraulic actuators, as a substitute if the active ride failed. For their development work on active ride, Lotus received the 1989 Charles Deutsch Prize, awarded 'to the company . . . who has designed an innovative process or application judged to be of the greatest potential value to the automotive industry today.'

No car with active ride was available to the public in the 1980s. But Nissan planned to offer a modified version on the Infiniti early in 1990, and Toyota on one model of the Celica coupé, to be followed by Mercedes-Benz on the SL roadster, and Chevrolet on the 1991 Corvette ZR1 using technology from GM-owned Lotus. However, a step in the same direction was taken by Rolls-Royce for the 1990 Silver Spirit. This had a computer-controlled adaptive damping system which worked on 'soft' up to 70 mph, 'normal' to 100 mph, and thereafter 'firm'. Mercedes-Benz and BMW had similar systems on their top models, but the Rolls-Royce control was more compact, being located in one black box under the dashboard, instead of distributed around the car.

ABS brakes

Developments in braking were similar to those in suspension, with 1960s technology (disc brakes) becoming much more widespread over the two decades. But the really important innovation arrived only in the second half of the 1980s. This was ABS (anti-lock braking system), which incorporated inductive wheel sensors that constantly measured the rotation speeds of all four wheels.

The moment a wheel was tending to lock, the electronic controller signalled to the ABS valve in that wheel, reducing brake pressure. This lasted only until the wheel was again rotating at a speed corres-

In the mid-1980s, an important innovation was born, the anti-lock braking system (ABS). This concept meant a lot for safety but, surprisingly, it was not standard equipment on all cars in 1990. Only the more luxurious family saloons had ABS as standard.

The system contains an electronic unit with sensors at all wheels, which registers if any of them tends to lock. Within a few milliseconds, the electronic ABS/TCS controller collects all the crucial information on driving forces (1), braking (2) and cornering (3) forces, normal forces (14), yawing moments about the vertical axis (5) and the moments of inertia of the wheels (6).

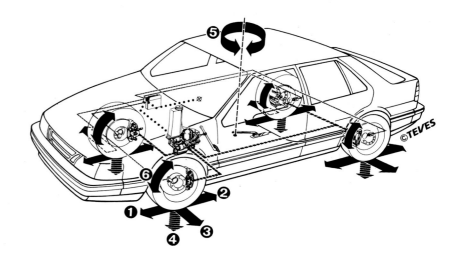

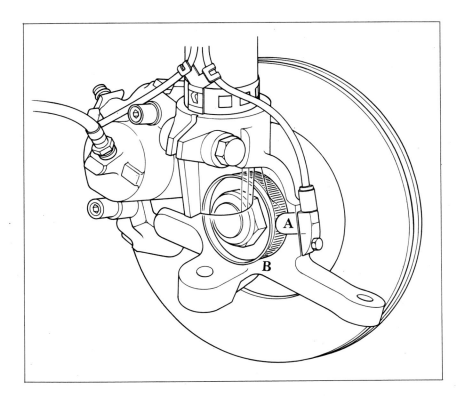

ABS on a front wheel. The speed sensor (A) goes into the steering knuckle, and the sensor placed near the toothed wheel (B) acts as an inductive voltage generator. The toothed wheel is mounted on splines in the hub, and rotates with the car wheel.

Pinto's petrol tank, which could lead to massive lawsuits from accident victims. The first widespread safety feature, and one of the simplest, was the seat belt, which was offered as long ago as 1952 by Nash and Muntz.

In 1970 one could still drive legally without a belt anywhere in the world. But in Britain and several other countries, they were mandatory fittings on all new cars, whether or not one chose to wear them. Compulsory use began in the Australian state of Victoria on 1 January 1971, and spread rapidly in the 1970s. By the end of our period, there were very few countries where belts were not obligatory. One was the United States, where the law varied from one state to another. They must be worn throughout Western Europe by front-seat passengers, although Italy did not make them compulsory until October 1989.

There are now moves to extend the rule to rear-seat passengers. Most Western European countries insist that new cars be fitted with rear seat belts, and they must be worn in Austria, Belgium, Finland, Germany, Norway and Sweden. In Britain they must be worn by children under 14. As for Eastern Europe . . .

ponding to the vehicle speed: then the brake pressure was either maintained or increased again. In the Teves ABS/TCS system, the front wheels were controlled independently, the rear wheels together. TCS (traction control system) had the effect of a limited-slip differential, reducing the speed of a spinning wheel until it could again transmit torque adequately.

Safety technology

'Safety doesn't sell cars' was long an unwritten rule of automobile marketing, and until the late 1960s little attention was paid to safety in advertising or promoting cars. Ralph Nader's determined crusade against the Chevrolet Corvair, which he dubbed 'unsafe at any speed', was not the main reason for the Corvair's demise. Yet manufacturers were becoming wary of design features, such as the Ford

The 1970s saw a number of ESV cars (Experimental Safety Vehicles), including this Volvo ESC (VESC) from 1972. The most striking things about such safety-cars were their big bumpers, mounted on telescopic shock absorbers to take the first blow of a collision. Note also the steel roll-bar on the roof.

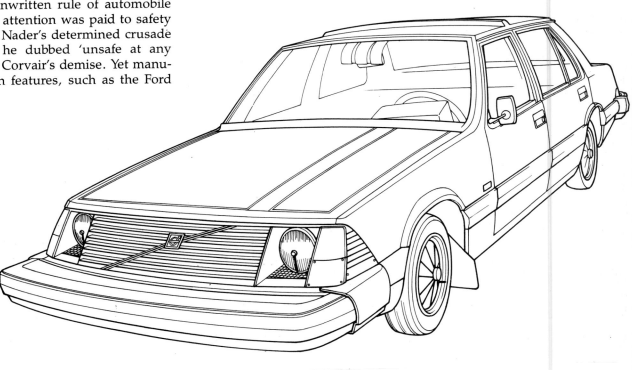

Experimental Safety Vehicles

In the early 1970s, designers began to pay more attention to safety in the cockpit, reducing the lethal areas against which a driver or passenger could be bruised or impaled. Features such as deep-dished steering wheels, energy-absorbing steering columns and padded dashboards began to appear. Externally, dangerous pedestrian-threatening mascots were eliminated.

The 1970s also saw a number of ESVs (Experimental Safety Vehicles), many of them grotesquely styled, in which safety took priority over appearance, aerodynamics or power-to-weight ratio. In June 1970, US Secretary of Transportation John Volpe offered multi-million dollar incentives to three companies to build ESVs. Only GM was an established car maker, the others being the Fairchild Corporation and AMF (American Machine & Foundry). Their brief was to build a four-door sedan with a maximum wheelbase of 124 inches and weight of 4,000 pounds, capable of withstanding 10-mph impacts front and rear with no deformation of the bumpers, and no damage to the passenger compartments at speeds up to 50 mph. The results were extraordinary to look at, the AMF being described as 'a double-ended battering ram', and the Fairchild having a front bumper that extended automatically 12 inches when the car's speed exceeded 25 mph.

The GM car was the most conventional of the three in appearance, though it featured a special frame and interior padding to give protection at impact speeds up to 30 mph – after which airbags would take over. Although not under contract, Ford also produced an ESV, a modified Galaxie. Other companies who joined the bandwagon over the next few years included Mercedes-Benz, Volkswagen, British Leyland, Volvo, Nissan and Toyota. Unfortunately, they were all

Experimental Safety Vehicles were seldom elegant, sacrificing style to passenger protection. Illustrated here are the Mercedes-Benz ESF-05 and the Fiat mini-ESV. Fiat's car was based on the 500, and it is hard to believe that the reinforced nose would give any protection at all.

Airbags were another safety device born in the late 1980s. When the car collides, the airbag inflates in about 40 milliseconds in front of the passenger, creating a protective zone. Shown here is an experiment at the Volvo Safety Laboratory.

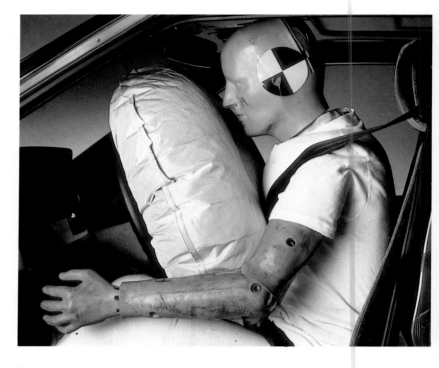

much heavier than production cars, and the fuel crisis of 1973/74 put an end to the ESVs, though several of their ideas were continued.

Airbags

The most persistent safety aid, invented in the 1960s and featured on all the American ESVs of the 1970s, was the airbag. In a collision, a chemical charge filled the bag with nitrogen–inflating it very rapidly, within about 40 milliseconds–and cushioned the passenger's body against injury by distributing the load of impact over as wide an area as possible. It then deflated gradually. Theoretically ideal in a head-on collision, it was only helpful within a range of 30 degrees on either side, and of no use at all in side or rear impacts, or in rollovers. There were also fears that the great increase in pressure might rupture passengers' eardrums, or blow out windows, though neither of these actually happened.

The airbag was most popular in America, where seat-belt wearing was slow to catch on, and not mandatory in all states. By the late 1980s, the airbag was a standard fitting on some of the US-market cars made by Ford, GM and Chrysler. Usually for the driver only, it was offered for the front passenger on some cars–although not yet for the rear passengers, who were thus protected on most of the 1970s ESVs. Imported cars which offered airbags were Audi, BMW, Mercedes-Benz and Volvo. British firms working on the idea in 1989 included Lotus, Rolls-Royce and Rover.

Safety begins to sell

Other, less dramatic, safety features appeared during the 1980s. Audi engineers, knowing that the steering column is the greatest threat to the driver, linked it with the engine/transmission, so that when this was forced back in a head-on collision, the steering wheel and column were tugged forward, away from the driver. Mercedes-Benz brought

out many safety ideas on the 1989 SL roadsters, including a rollbar which popped up automatically if the car's angle suggested an imminent rollover–and tensioning of the seat belts at the moment of impact, using inertia sensors and a controlled explosion to drive a tiny turbine attached to the belt reel.

The SL also came with run-flat tyres capable of being driven up to 190 miles at a maximum of 50 mph, even after a puncture. The 1986 Jaguar XJ6 had U-section plates fitted to the lower part of the doors and the sills: in a side collision the two plates interlocked, clamping the door to the sill, giving greatly increased strength.

All the foregoing safety devices have represented cure rather than prevention, coping with the results of a collision rather than preventing one from happening. However, there was great progress in this field too, thanks to anti-lock braking and the improvements in transmission and suspension mentioned earlier. In all respects, the car of 1989 was a much safer vehicle than its predecessor of 1969.

2
INTERNATIONAL TRENDS AND NATIONAL CHARACTERISTICS

Forty years ago, most cars displayed marked national characteristics. British family cars had long-stroke engines and conservative styling, while the sports cars were traditional, not to say archaic. French and Italian cars were nervous and high-revving, with advanced suspensions to cope with poor roads–whereas American cars were softly sprung, wallowing gas-guzzlers. Japanese cars were unknown outside Japan.

The first twenty years after World War II saw a gradual blurring of these differences. But in the past two decades they have almost completely disappeared, not only because the optimum shape and specification for a car have become increasingly standardized, wherever the car is designed, but because the same designs are made in many countries. Thus a Pontiac Le Mans was really an Opel Kadett made in Korea, while Toyota Camrys were made in the USA for export to Japan–and Honda Legends were made in both Britain and Japan, as were their British counterparts, the Rover 800s.

Western Europe

Although internationalism became rampant in the 1970s, there had been some degree of cross-border manufacture for a long time. Cit-

roens and Renaults were both assembled in Britain in the 1950s, while Simca began life as a French-made Fiat in the 1930s, and Fiats were made by NSU in Germany at various times between 1931 and 1973.

Nevertheless, in 1970 there was quite a lot of individuality even between the marques of the multi-national companies, Ford, General Motors and Chrysler. If Ford's Escort and Capri were already Anglo-German cars, the bigger Zephyr from Britain and 26M from Germany still had distinctive styling and engineering. The larger Vauxhalls were still different from Opels, while the products of Chrysler Europe were still descendants of the old companies which Chrysler had acquired: Britain's Hillman Imp, Minx and Humber Sceptre, and France's Simca 1000, 1100 and 1500.

GM Europe

All this was to change within the next ten years, thanks to rationalization and the introduction of international cars, as Europe's industries combined to combat the growing threat from Japan. In 1974 General Motors brought out the Chevette, a three-door hatchback originally made in Brazil–and later in the USA, Britain (Vauxhall Chevette), Germany (Opel Kadett) and Japan (Isuzu Gemini).

The next-generation Opel Kadett was made in Britain as the Vauxhall Astra. With the arrival of the front-drive J-car, badged in Britain as a Vauxhall Cavalier, in Germany as an Opel Ascona, and in Australia as a Holden Camira–as well as being made by all of

The first truly international car was GM's Chevette, which was launched by their Brazilian division in 1974. Next came the Vauxhall Chevette in 1975, the Opel Kadett, American Chevette and Isuzu Gemini in 1976. The latter was sold in Australia as the Holden Gemini. Illustrated is a Chevette GL of the late 1970s. American Chevettes lasted longer than European ones, which gave way to the front-drive Opel Kadett/Vauxhall Astra in 1984. The design was still made in Brazil in 1989, in notchback form.

General Motors' J-car was made in Britain as the Vauxhall Cavalier, in Germany as the Opel Ascona, in Australia as the Holden Camira—while in America all five divisions had their own versions (see page 188, caption to Cadillac Cimarron). Engine options in the European cars ran from an economy-sized 1297 cc up to 1998 cc, and included a 1598-cc diesel. The American J-cars were offered with 1796 or 1998 cc only, both with fuel injection. Shown here is a 1984 Vauxhall Cavalier 1600L. Bodies were completely restyled for 1988.

America's GM divisions–individuality dwindled further. The process was completed by the Spanish-built Vauxhall Nova/Opel Corsa, and the larger saloons badged as Vauxhall Carlton/Opel Omega and the Senator, which carried the same name in both countries.

By 1988 there were no specifically British Vauxhalls, and not all the models were even made in Britain, their sources being as follows: Nova built at Zaragoza, Spain; Astra built at Ellesmere Port, Cheshire, except for GTE 16-valve and convertibles, which came from Germany (Opel and Karmann); Cavalier built at Luton, Bedfordshire, except for 4×4 and GSi2000 which were made by Opel; Carlton and Senator, all made by Opel.

Ford Europe

A similar situation prevailed at Ford. The Fiesta was an international car, with engines made in Spain (950 and 1100) and Britain (1400 and 1600), transmissions in France, body panels and assembly in Britain, Germany and Spain. Even a British-assembled Fiesta had probably no more than 70% British-made components. Sierras and Sapphires were assembled in Britain and Belgium, their engines being sourced from Britain (1400 and 1600), America (1800) and Germany (1800 and V6). The 2.3-litre diesel engine was supplied by Peugeot. Transmissions came from Britain and France. The top-of-the-line Scorpio (Granada in Britain) was made only in Germany.

Chrysler Europe

The Chrysler name disappeared in Europe after 1978, when Peugeot acquired the Chrysler Alpine and Horizon models–which were built in the former Rootes Group factory at Coventry, and the Simca factory at Poissy. Peugeot renamed the cars Talbots, and brought out two new models: the large Tagora saloon in 1981, and the Peugeot 104-based Samba hatchback and convertible in 1982.

Neither sold as well as hoped for, and in 1986 the Talbot name was dropped. The Poissy factory was added to Peugeot's stock, and the Coventry plant was given over to manufacture of Peugeot 309s. This was yet another foreign design being made in Britain, others being Hondas by British Leyland (now Austin Rover) and Nissans at their own factory in Sunderland.

Peugeot-Citroen and Renault

Rationalization also took place within the French industry, following Peugeot's acquisition of Citroen in 1974. This resulted in a hybrid design called the Visa, a Peugeot 104 body-shell powered by Citroen's air-cooled flat-twin engine. This survived until 1988, with 4-cylinder engines being added. A derivative was made in Rumania under the name Oltcit, and exported to France as the Axel. The Peugeot-Citroen merger meant that there were only two volume car producers in France, the other being the state-owned Renault company.

The two groups cooperated in the design and manufacture of the Douvrin engine, named after the factory where it was made. Introduced in 1974, this 2664-cc V6 unit, also known as the PRV (Peugeot-Renault-Volvo) went into the Peugeot 504 coupé and 604 saloon, Renault 30 and Volvo 264. Outside the triumvirate which developed it, the Douvrin engine was used by John De Lorean for his controversial coupé, and in the Scottish-built Argyll GT coupé. Enlarged to

The Chrysler name was lost to European cars after 1978, when the troubled American company sold out to Peugeot. The former Chrysler Horizon (Simca Horizon in France) was renamed a Talbot Horizon, and continued under that name until 1985. It was a five-door hatchback in the Golf or Escort class, and was available with a 1.9-litre diesel engine from 1982, also being made in the USA as the Dodge Omni or Plymouth Horizon. Illustrated is a 1984 Talbot Horizon 1.4-litre LS model (left).

In 1974 three companies—Peugeot, Renault and Volvo—joined forces to design and manufacture the Douvrin engine. This, among others, went into the Renault 30 (above) and Peugeot 504 coupé and cabriolet. Illustrated is the standard version of 504.

2849 cc for 1981, it powered the Peugeot 505 as well as 604 in the 1980s, the Renault 25 and Alpine GTA rear-engined coupé, and the Volvo 760/780 saloons and coupés.

Looking for national characteristics, one could still discern these in the Citroen range, from the evergreen 2CV with its interconnected coil suspension (made only in Portugal since 1987) to the advanced XM with the most sophisticated suspension in any European car. By the 1980s, the French sports car was limited to the Renault-built Alpine GTA and the limited production MVS coupé with Renault V6 engine.

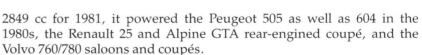

In 1981 the PRV engine was enlarged to 2849 cc and put into the Volvo 760/780. Seen here is a 760 saloon (left).

43

The Citroen CX was replaced in 198_
by the XM, which had an even more
sophisticated suspension system tha_
its predecessor (see page 156). As always, the design and construction u_
advanced, and it was appointed "Ca_
the Year" in 1989. It had a transver_
3-litre V6 driving the front wheels, _
maximum output was 170 bhp at
5,600 rpm.

Something typically French

Another typically French car, with a tradition dating back to bef_
1914, was the cyclecar–or in its recent manifestation, the microc_
This took advantage of the fact that a vehicle whose engine capac_
did not exceed 50 cc could be driven without any form of licence, a_
could be taxed and insured very cheaply. Charles Mochet had ma_
such cars in the 1950s, and twenty years later a crop of them enter_
the market.

One of the first was the Riboud, made as a 3- or 4-wheeler, with _
cc Sachs single-cylinder engine, 2-speed automatic transmission a_

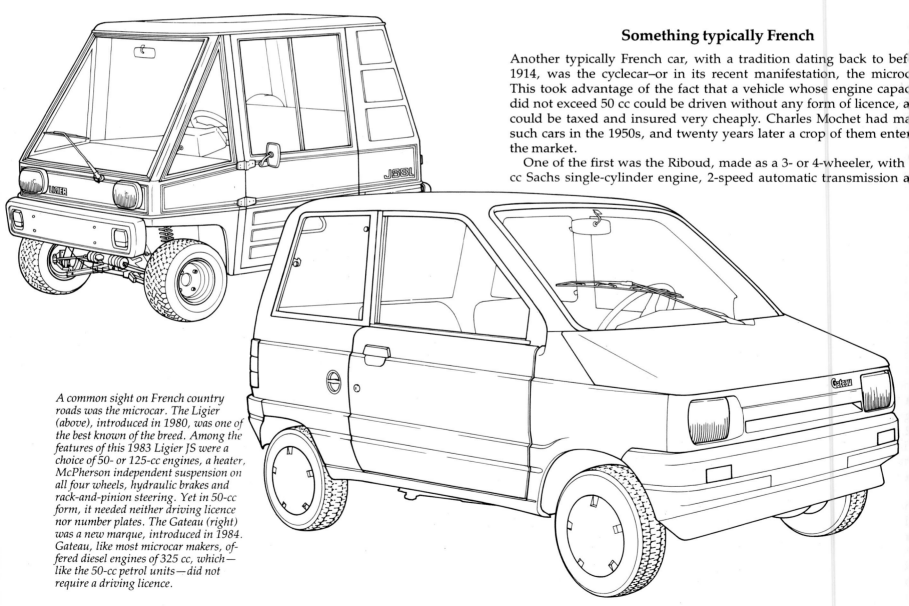

A common sight on French country
roads was the microcar. The Ligier
(above), introduced in 1980, was one of
the best known of the breed. Among the
features of this 1983 Ligier JS were a
choice of 50- or 125-cc engines, a heater,
McPherson independent suspension on
all four wheels, hydraulic brakes and
rack-and-pinion steering. Yet in 50-cc
form, it needed neither driving licence
nor number plates. The Gateau (right)
was a new marque, introduced in 1984.
Gateau, like most microcar makers, offered diesel engines of 325 cc, which—
like the 50-cc petrol units—did not
require a driving licence.

disc brakes on the rear wheels. The Riboud lasted until 1981, by which time it had been joined by at least fifteen rival makes. Among the better-known were the box-like Ligier from the racing-car makers; the Duport, which pioneered the use of diesel engines in microcars; Bellier, Erad, Marden and Microcar.

During the 1980s there was an inevitable elimination of the less successful companies, and in 1988 only eleven makers were listed out of the forty or so which had flitted across the scene. Most of them widened their market by offering larger engines, up to 400 cc, in the same body-shells. Diesel engines up to 325 cc could be operated without a driving licence, being limited, like the petrol models, to a maximum speed of 45 mph.

Microcars appealed particularly to retired folk in country districts, who covered a limited mileage and seldom ventured beyond the local market town. They were hardly ever seen in large cities. Most were pretty fragile and breakdowns were frequent, particularly in the transmission department. Nor were they especially cheap: a 1989 Ligier 325-cc cost FF 52,000, more than a 5-door Citroen AX or a basic Peugeot 205. Even the cheapest 1989 micro, the Erad Capucine, cost FF 1000 more than a Citroen 2CV.

Ford takes over Jaguar and Aston Martin

In Britain the specialist car flourished up to the end of the 1980s, although the massive investment needed for new models forced three of the best-known names into the hands of foreign multi-nationals. Towards the end of 1985, Lotus–in which Toyota already had a 21% stake–was acquired by General Motors, and two years later Ford took control of Aston Martin. Most surprising of all, though to informed observers an inevitable step, was Ford's take-over of Jaguar in November 1989.

The Coventry firm found itself in an increasingly competitive market, fighting for sales against much larger and richer BMW and Mercedes-Benz, who had cheaper and smaller cars to generate investment capital. When Nissan and Toyota moved into the field at the beginning of 1989, the competition became stiffer still; and without a massive outside injection of capital, Jaguar could never have developed the essential new models, including a smaller car to rival the BMW 5 Series. Fears that Ford will compromise Jaguar quality seem unfounded, for the American company will value their new acquisition as a way into an important specialist field. Jaguar will be to Ford as Lexus is to Toyota and Infiniti to Nissan.

An interesting question was what General Motors would do to match Ford. There were no suitable and available European companies for them to acquire, but an upgrading of the top Opels on the lines of the Lotus-developed Omega seemed to be one answer.

Jaguar, with sales around 50,000, were in the middle of the production league, but several British firms got by satisfactorily on less than a tenth of that figure. Rolls-Royce, after a late-1970s dip in sales, gradually worked up their deliveries to 2,238 in 1984, 2,551 in 1985, 2,784 in 1987 and 2,801 in 1988. Rolls were backed up by the massive financial muscle of the Vickers Group, but several British firms who had to stand on their own also survived the 1980s on annual sales of less than 1000.

Morgan and TVR both bought engines and many other components from outside, thereby taking advantage of the research and development of their suppliers (particularly the Rover V8 engine), instead of spending the money themselves. Of other firms, Panther survived only because of a take-over by a large Korean firm, while Reliant have struggled through the 1980s with diminishing sales, supplementing their income with sub-contract work such as assembling

Under the British Leyland regime, the more innovative front-drive cars were badged as Austins, while the Morris name went on the very conventional Marina and its successor, the Ital. Shown here is a 1978 Austin Allegro, the successor to the long-lived 1100/1300 series using the same engines (and two larger ones), though Hydragas instead of Hydralastic suspension—in a body which was completely restyled, but not for the better. Early models had an unusual quartic steering wheel (four gentle arcs joined together). This was thought appropriate for the car's high-tech image, but journalists and customers disliked it, and it was dropped within a few years. The Allegro was made from 1973 to 1983, but never sold as well as its predecessors.

the 200 Ford RS200 rally cars and, more recently, taking on manufacture of the Metrocab taxicab.

The Rover Group

The only survivor of the once great British volume car industry was British Leyland, now the Rover Group. The British Leyland Motor Corporation was formed in 1968 through a merger between the British Motor Holdings (Austin, Jaguar, MG, Morris, Riley, Wolseley) and Leyland Motors, who owned Standard-Triumph and Rover as well as several truck makers. They entered the 1970s with a vast range of models and much duplication of resources and management–and though a profit of £58 million was recorded in 1973, a combination of rising oil prices, falling demand for cars and serious industrial unrest hit the company very hard. Between 1968 and 1975 their share of the UK market fell from 40 to 30% and exports declined by 35%.

In order to prevent the whole concern going under, the British Government agreed to provide the necessary working capital, taking 95% of the shares of the company–which was reconstituted as British Leyland Ltd. At first the cars continued as before, with the innovative front-drive models such as the Allegro and Maxi being sold under the Austin badge (the Mini had been a marque of its own since 1970) and the conventional rear-drive models (Marina) being badged as Morrises.

Jaguar suffered the indignity of becoming the Large Car Division of Leyland Cars from 1975 to 1978, when the new boss Michael Edwardes realized the importance of individuality and made it part of Jaguar-Rover-Triumph Ltd. However, MG was starved of funds as money for sports cars was spent on the Triumph TR7. The result was that MG disappeared in 1980, and the TR7 did not survive beyond 1981, due to sales resistance in the USA.

The first fruit of collaboration between British Leyland and Honda was the Triumph Acclaim (left) of 1981–84. Advertised as 'Totally Equipped to Triumph', it was a Honda Ballade assembled in Britain with Japanese engine and transmission. It paved the way for the next generation, also Ballade-based, which were badged as Rover 200s. These had a single bodyshell but two engines: a 1342-cc Honda in the 213, and a 1598-cc Leyland O Series in the 216 (lower left). Power steering was an option not available on the Rovers. For 1990 the 213/216 were joined, though eventually to be replaced by, the Honda Concerto-based 214/216—with Rover 1.4-litre twin-overhead-camshaft, or Honda 1.6-litre single-overhead-camshaft, engine.

English cars with Japanese engines

Triumph was the first BL marque to be linked with Honda. Lacking the funds needed to develop a new medium-sized quality car, BL chose the Honda Ballade, initially as a stop-gap until they could develop their own. Engine and transmission were made by Honda, the Honda-styled body shell was made by Pressed Steel at Cowley, and final assembly took place at the old Morris Motors factory at Cowley. The rather bland four-door saloon was called the Triumph Acclaim, and sold 133,000 units before it was replaced in 1984 by another Honda-based car, the Rover 200.

By now, BL had given up the idea of developing their own car in this class. The Rovers, one with a 1342-cc Honda engine (213) and the

other with a 1598-cc Leyland engine (216), were made until 1989 when they were replaced by the Honda Concerto-based 200s, using Rover's new 1.4-litre twin-cam K engine or a 1.6-litre single-cam Honda unit. This important new range replaced the previous Rover 200s, and will eventually replace the Austin Maestro; the Montego will give way to the booted Rover 400 in 1990. As the larger Rover 800s are also Honda-based (Legend), this means that apart from the ageing Mini, the Rover Group's only British-designed car will be the Metro.

Honda's involvement extends beyond the Rover models, as the Concerto is built by Rover's Longbridge factory for export to EEC countries, and in 1989 Honda set up their own engine plant at Swindon. For a while, the Honda Legend was built at Cowley and the

The first factory to make purely Japanese designs in Britain was set up by Nissan at Washington, Tyne & Wear in 1986. The car was the Bluebird, initially a saloon and joined by a hatchback one year later. This is a 1988 Turbo ZX hatchback with 115-mph top speed. Of the 70,000 Washington cars made in 1989, about 30,000 were exported. Other EEC countries regard them—somewhat reluctantly—as British because of the substantial proportion (by value) of British-made components.

Rover 800 in Japan—but this came to an end in March 1988, as the proposed changes in both models would not have been compatible with joint production.

The 800 was sold in the USA as the Sterling, with no Rover badging, in order to avoid reminders of the unsuccessful US career of the Rover SD1. However, they were plagued with quality problems, and Sterling sales have dropped alarmingly, form 14,000 in 1987 to 8,822 in 1988, and the prospects for 1989 likely to be still lower. By contrast, Honda sold 70,770 Legends in the USA in 1988, under their brand name Acura.

Japanese cars made in Britain

A different form of Japanese involvement in the British motor industry came in 1986, when Nissan set up a factory at Washington, Tyne & Wear, for the manufacture of the Bluebird saloon. A hatchback was added in 1987, when production reached 24,000 cars. This rose to 56,541 in 1988, and by 1992 Nissan hoped to be making 200,000 cars annually, half of Bluebird size and half of Micra size. If these figures are achieved, Nissan could be the third largest UK car producers,

after Ford and Rover. Further Japanese involvement was announced in 1989, with a proposed Toyota factory near Derby.

Despite these foreign ventures, Britain's share of world production dropped alarmingly during three decades. In 1960 she was in third place, beaten only by the USA and Germany. Ten years later she was fifth, overtaken by Japan and France—while in 1988 she was eighth, behind Italy, Spain and the Soviet Union as well her previous rivals. Imports were at record levels, being over 50% throughout the 1980s, the highest proportion of any of the world's major manufacturing countries. The 1985 figure was 58%, but if the proportion of foreign-made components in British cars was taken into account (Volkswagen gearboxes in Maestros and Montegos, for example), the true figure, by value, was closer to 66%.

The Alfasud (above) marked several firsts for this Italian company. It was their first car with front-wheel drive and a flat-four engine, and the first to be built away from Milan—namely at Pomigliano d'Arco near Naples. More than 826,000 were made, from 1971 to 1984, including over 102,000 Sprint coupes styled by Ital Design. This is a 1982 five-door hatchback. It was replaced by the larger and heavier 33—and also by the unloved Arna, which used Alfasud running gear in a Nissan Cherry body.

Fiat had great success in the 1980s, and was at the top of the European car production chart for several years. Two models which contributed to their success were the Panda and Tipo (left). New for 1988, the Tipo was a contender in the highly competitive Ford Escort/VW Golf market. Much of the body was galvanized steel, which put an end to Fiat's reputation for rust-prone cars. Engine options were a wide variety, from 1108 to 1995 cc, including a diesel and a turbo diesel.

In Italy, Fiat buys up everything

The trend towards ever larger conglomerates was seen in other European countries. Fiat, which had dominated Italian production since the 1920s, took an even bigger share by the acquisition of Lancia in 1969 and Alfa Romeo in 1986. Their take-over of Ferrari in 1969 did not add much to their volume of cars produced (less than 4,000 per year), but it gave them a base in the supercar bracket and in Formula 1 racing.

There was much less foreign involvement in the Italian industry than in the British. It was mainly confined to the use of Daihatsu 3-cylinder engines in the Innocenti 990 since 1982, the joint Alfa Romeo-Nissan ARNA project, Chrysler's 1987 acquisition of Lamborghini and, most importantly, the Group 4 cars shared between Fiat, Alfa Romeo, Lancia and Saab.

The ARNA (Alfa Romeo Nissan Automobiles) was an attempt to provide a cut-price replacement for the Alfasud, by combining the body-shell of a Nissan Cherry with an Alfasud engine of 1½ litre and transmission. It was not a success, looking too much like a Cherry which catered for a different market than the more sporting Alfasud, while the Italian-built Cherry bodies lacked the quality of the Japanese versions. Neither Nissan nor Alfa dealers liked selling it, and

production ended in 1985 after about 50,000 had been made.

The Type 4 cars were an interesting example of shared designs to reduce development costs, on the same lines as the PRV Douvrin engine. First to appear was the Lancia Thema, in Autumn 1984, followed by the Saab 9000, the Fiat Croma in December 1985 and the Alfa Romeo 164 in autumn 1987. Details are given in Chapter 2.

Fiat—biggest in Europe

Fiat had an extremely successful decade, being the leading European producer for several years, with factories working at 97% of capacity, compared with 88–89% average for other European plants. They also had thirteen assembly plants in other countries, as well as providing technology for several marques in different countries. These included Yugoslavia (Yugo), Spain until 1980 (Seat), Poland (Polski-Fiat), the Soviet Union (Lada) and India (Premier).

In 1989 they seemed poised to extend their empire northwards, by taking some stake in the troubled Saab company—while at home they were likely to take over Maserati. There were also rumours in 1989 of technical collaboration with Mercedes-Benz, following a link in the fields of communications and military hardware.

In contrast to Britain and Italy, the German motor industry seemed immune to foreign involvement, apart from the presence of Ford and General Motors which had existed for decades. International collaboration took the form of exporting German technology, either in

actual manufacture, such as that of Volkswagen in Spain, Yugoslavia, China and Japan, or consultancy in the form of Porsche's work on the Spanish Seat. Apart from the brief manufacture of the Rover 800 under Honda auspices, VW was the only foreign company to make cars in Japan.

Germany – the last resort

Germany was the only European country to have no speed limits, on certain motorways. This led to the development of very fast cars–not only luxury saloons and roadsters such as the Mercedes-Benz 560SL, but creations of tuning companies which boosted the already massive power of Italian supercars still further. A Koenig-tuned Ferrari BB512 with twin Rajay turbochargers developed 653 bhp, nearly double the output of the engine when it left Maranello, and gave a top speed of over 200 mph.

There were also some home-grown supercars, such as the 5.6-litre Mercedes-Benz-powered Isdera Imperator with top speed of 180 mph, and the Zender Visions and Fact, also mid-engined coupés with Audi or Mercedes-Benz power. The Zenders were made by a well-known tuning and accessory firm, and have yet to enter production. However, by the end of the 1980s, a question mark hung over the future of high-performance cars in Germany.

The Isdera Imperator from 1988 was the German answer to Lamborghini's Countach. It was constructed by Eberhard Schultz, a pleasant surprise in the car world during the later 1980s. The Imperator had a 5547-cc V8 engine from Mercedes, and its output was said to be 390 bhp at 5,500 rpm. Top speed was 179 mph.

It seemed that political pressure might lead to overall speed limits–and to forestall this, most manufacturers apart from Porsche agreed to limit their top speeds to 155 mph. Projects such as the 48-valve V12 engine for the BMW 850i coupé might well be shelved. BMW's own chief engineer, Hans-Peter Weisbarth, said "This nonsense has to stop somewhere; someone has to stop the horsepower race. We must regulate ourselves ... for otherwise we will let the politicians decide."

The BMW coupé might not have been built for political reasons—or so this author thought when writing the main text of the present book. But it was! BMW just didn't listen to growing protests over the horsepower race. The 850i coupe had the same V12 engine as the 750i model.

SEAT made a habit of building four-door versions of Fiats which the Turin factory made only in two-door form. These included the 600, 850 and 127. Here is a 1970 Especial 850 saloon.

The mid-1980s saw a new range of SEAT cars which owed nothing to Fiat designs. Their single-overhead-camshaft 4-cylinder engines were Porsche-designed, and the bodies were styled by Ital Design's Giugiaro. First to appear was the Ibiza three-door hatchback (left), later made in five-door form, followed by the booted Malaga saloon. Engine options are 903-, 1193- and 1461-cc petrol, and 1714-cc diesel. In 1989 SEAT was still making a Fiat design, the Panda-inspired Marbella, and VW Polos.

Spain – an unknown car nation

The Spanish industry enjoyed tremendous growth in post-war years, exceeded only by Japan. In 1947 they turned out 68 cars and 119 commercial vehicles; forty-one years later, they were the seventh largest motor manufacturer in the world and the fourth largest in Western Europe, making 1,497,967 cars and 368,437 commercial vehicles.

Many of these were international designs built for export, such as the Ford Fiesta and the small GM car sold as a Vauxhall Nova or Opel Corsa. Seat underwent a great change in the 1980s, when their long-standing ties with Fiat were broken, largely because the Spanish government would not agree to Fiat's demand for cutbacks at the over-manned Seat factories.

The government invested heavily in new models, still Fiat-based. But from 1982 Volkswagen became increasingly involved in Seat, with Polos, Passats and Santanas being assembled in Barcelona, while 1985 saw a new range of cars with Porsche-designed single-overhead-camshaft engines and bodies styled by Giugiaro. These were the Ibiza hatchback and the Malaga saloon, which have enjoyed considerable export sales as well as being in third or fourth place on the home market.

Since entering the EEC, Spain has seen an enormous growth in imported cars. In 1988, sales rose by 5% for locally-built cars and by 47% for imports. Key foreign companies with a foothold in Spanish industry include Renault, Land Rover and Suzuki; all European-market small 4×4 Suzukis are Spanish-built.

Sweden: GM takes over Saab

Sweden's motor industry has seen steady, if unspectacular, growth over the past two decades–from 278,971 cars in 1970 to 407,117 in 1988. The same two companies have contributed to these totals, Volvo and Saab, with the former taking about four-fifths of the domestic market in recent years. Estimated 1988 figures were 126,000 Saabs and 420,000 Volvos, the latter figure including 120,000 Dutch-built 300 and 400 series.

Saab had a Finnish factory where some special models were made exclusively, such as the 99 long-wheelbase limousine and the 900 convertible, as well as other models for the Finnish market. Volvo's overseas plants included one at Halifax, Canada, which built about 10,000 740s annually, around 10% of the total North American market–and another in South Korea, set up in 1989 with a first-year target of 7,000 240s, and anticipated production of 40,000 cars per year by 1995.

In 1989 Saab ran into trouble, with a loss of £80 million in the first half of the year. Being a medium-sized firm, they needed large sums for research and development–and like Jaguar, they could only find this through a link with a multi-national. Ford were talked of as a possible saviour, but by November it seemed that a more likely partner was to be Fiat. The latter, after all, were already linked with Saab in production of the 9000, one of the Type 4 cars. Yet early in 1990 the deal was to be closed with General Motors–soon followed by a gigantic merger of Volvo with Renault.

One of the special Saab models made in the company's Finnish factory at Nystad was the Turbo 16 cabriolet (top), launched in 1986. Another 'finnish' model was the 99, still made in small numbers. As a result of the GM takeover of Saab, it was announced that the Opel Calibra coupe will be built in the Nystad factory from 1991 onward.

The Volvo 460, introduced late in 1989, was a booted version of the 440, and aimed at the ''compact prestige'' market. Like the 440 and 480, it was by Volvo in the Netherlands. It also shared those cars' power train and platform, while the 1721-cc engine came with either carburettor, fuel injection or turbo.

Eastern Europe

The rate of development in Soviet Bloc countries has been much slower than in the west. Old-fashioned designs sold well enough in countries where there was nothing else to buy, while they also found adequate markets in Western Europe among unsophisticated motorists who were attracted by their low price. The more popular cars were those derived from Western models, such as Russia's Lada and Poland's Polski-Fiat, both inspired by the Fiat 124.

In Russia there was a waiting list of several years for a Lada, even in the late 1980s, but the unloved Moskvitch 412 could be bought virtually off the showroom floor. In 1970 the Moskvitch 408 had a 1357-cc pushrod overhead-valve engine, and did not even boast synchromesh on all its forward speeds. A 1478-cc single-overhead-camshaft engine and all-synchromesh came on the 412, but this still had the same high build and poor handling, and was made with little change right up to 1989.

It was joined in 1987 by two new models, developed with the aid of Renault: the IZH-4126 and the Moskvitch 2141. These had similar five-door hatchback bodies, but the IZH (named after the factory at Izhvesk where it was made) had the same 1478-cc engine as the 412 driving the rear wheels, while the 2141 (sold in Western Europe as the Aleko) had front drive and the option of a 1569-cc engine.

The Soviet Union: a runner-up

The Lada story is a close parallel to that of the Moskvitch, though the cars always had a better reputation. Known in their own country as

VAZ (Volzhsky Avtomobilny Zavod = Volga Automobile Works), they were introduced in 1969, being Fiat 124s with 1198-cc single-overhead-camshaft engines in place of the Fiat's pushrod unit. Apart from that, and the provision of a starting handle and a very efficient heater, they were very similar to the Fiat.

With several enlargements of engine, up to 1570 cc, this car has been made until 1989, receiving an optional five-speed gearbox or three-speed automatic in 1986. However, it was joined (Russian manufacturers never replace one model with another, always allowing an overlap of several years between old and new) in 1987 by an all-new hatchback in the Western mould, with transverse single-overhead-camshaft engines driving the front wheels. Engines were of 1100, 1300 and 1500 cc, and there were three- or five-door models. Known in Russia as the VAZ-2108 and on export markets as the Shiguli or Lada Samara, it seems set to win many more friends than any of its predecessors, though quality control is still not up to Western standards.

Traditional Russian cars made through-out the 1970s and 1980s were the Moskvitch 412 (right) and VAZ Lada (centre), the latter seen here in its estate-car version VAZ-2102. The Moskvitch was a home-grown car descended from a 1956 design, whereas the more popular Lada was a Fiat 124 with its own single-overhead-camshaft engine. Among other differences from the Fiat were the provision of a starting handle and a very effective heater. This could create an in-car temperature of 25° C when the weather outside was as cold as −25° C. Lada production in 1984 totalled 722,744 cars.

The late 1980s saw much more up-to-date designs from Russian factories. The Moskvitch 2141 (right), sold in Western markets as the Aleko, was a front-drive five-door hatchback with 1478- or 1569-cc longitudinal engine. The same bodyshell was used for the rear-drive IZH-2126.

The 'baby car' of the Russian industry was the ZAZ, or Zaporozhets, a two-door saloon with air-cooled V4 engine. First made in 1960, it was exported under the name Yalta during the early 1970s, when it had a water-cooled in-line Renault engine. But most have been sold on the home market, where the V4 engine of 1196 cc was still employed in 1989 (above). An eventual replacement, with greater export potential, was the Tauria 1102 (left), a three-door hatchback in the contemporary Western mode, with transverse engine driving the front wheels. Exports are expected to begin in 1990.

Russia's medium-sized car was the GAZ-3102 (left), known familiarly as the Volga and made in various forms since 1955. This current model, produced since 1982, is powered by a 2446-cc 4-cylinder pushrod overhead-valve engine with three valves per cylinder. It is also available with an 8-valve engine, with a 2304-cc Peugeot Indenor diesel engine, and with more old-fashioned saloon and estate bodies.

After years of making ill-handling rear-engined cars, Skoda came up to date in 1987 with the Favorit, a front-engined five-door hatchback with 1289-cc transverse engine driving the front wheels. A five-speed gearbox was featured, and in 1989 Skoda became the first manufacturer from the Eastern Bloc to offer a catalytic converter on their cars.

Built in the Polski-Fiat factory, the Polonez of 1979 was a half-modern design, with a five-door hatchback body on the old Fiat 125-based running gear. Since 1981 all Polski-Fiat products have gone under the name FSO, apart from the little rear-engined 126 which is called FSM and made in a separate factory from the larger cars. In fact, all Fiat 126s have been made in Poland since 1979.

Russia's 'baby car', the rear-engined Zaporozhets, was made with little change throughout the period, and was exported only briefly. In 1988 it was also joined by a new model, the Tauria three-door hatchback, with a front-mounted transverse 1091-cc engine driving the front wheels. Thus in the space of three years, the Soviet industry has three new and up-to-date models with which to compete on export markets. They are undoubtedly more serious competitors than ever before, and production has risen from 344, 248 in 1970 to 1,318,866 in 1988, putting them slightly ahead of Great Britain.

Czechoslovakia and Poland

A similar story can be told of other car-producing Eastern Bloc countries. In Czechoslovakia the old rear-engined Skoda 1000, though

improved in handling during the 1970s, sold mainly on its low price. In 1988 it was joined by a more modern design in the fashionable hatchback mould, with transverse 1289-cc single-overhead-camshaft engine driving the front wheels, five-speed gearbox and Bertone styling. In 1989, it became the first car from Eastern Europe to come with a catalytic comverter.

Poland's ancient Polski-Fiat 125 was joined in 1979 by the Polonez, which featured a five-door hatchback on the 125's running gear. Two years later, the name of all products was changed to FSO (Fabryka Samochodow Osobowych), at least on export markets where Fiat objected to the possible confusion of their cars with the Polish product. A modern front-drive hatchback is in the offing, but has not yet been announced.

Another Polish factory, FSM (Fabryka Samochodow Malolit-

razowych) built the 2-cylinder rear-engined Fiat 126. For the last ten years, all 126s for Western Europe as well as East have been sourced from Poland. Its successor, code-named X1/79, is planned for introduction in 1996, with production of at least 260,000 per year, of which about 35% would be exported to EEC countries. The Polish industry also built the old-fashioned Syrena with 842-cc vertical 3-cylinder engine and front-wheel drive. Introduced in 1955 as a 2-cylinder 2-stroke, it lasted until the mid-1980s.

Yugoslavia

Yugoslavia is another country which has built its industry on obsolete Fiat models. The Zastava factory began by assembling 1400s in 1954, and until 1981 it built the rear-engined 600 abandoned by Fiat in 1970.

The 101 was based on Fiat's transverse-engined front-drive 128, but had the advantage of a hatchback, which was never obtainable from Turin. Dropped by Fiat in 1984, it was still made in Yugoslavia in 1989, under the name Yugo 513.

Other models, which all carried the brand name Yugo, were the 45/55 (a re-skinned Fiat 127, with 127 overhead-valve or 128-type single-overhead-camshaft engines), and the brand new Giugiaro-styled five-door hatchback launched as the Florida and renamed Sana (after a Yugoslav river). This was in the same class as the Fiat Tipo, and had a transverse 1372-cc Fiat engine, with larger versions expected in the 1990s. It was Yugoslavia's first up-to-date car to compete in world markets. Whereas previous Yugos had sold on the strength of their low prices, the Sana was more seriously competitive with Western rivals.

Alone among East European cars, the ancient products of the German Democratic Republic had no modern developments waiting in the wings at the end of 1989. The only major change was that the smoky two-stroke engines finally gave way to four-stroke VW Polo units, on the Wartburg (right) in autumn 1988, and on the Trabant (above right) in November 1989. The latter was too late for the thousands of Trabants which poured across the borders into Hungary and West Germany after controls were relaxed. The Bundestag passed special legislation to let the polluting two-strokes enter its country, but the border police were not pleased, claiming that the fumes caused nausea and sore throats. About 146,000 Trabants were made in 1989, representing 70% of East German car production. The rest were Wartburgs.

East Germany: nothing happening

Thus Yugoslavia, Czechoslovakia and the Soviet Union all had up-to-date cars entering the 1990s, with Poland likely to announce one soon. The glaring exception was East Germany, whose antiquated two-stroke engined Trabant and Wartburg were continued throughout the 1970s and 1980s with very little change—though the Wartburg gained front disc brakes in 1974, and in 1988 the old two-stroke finally gave way to a VW Polo engine.

At the beginning of the 1990s, there was no sign of any replacements. Yet the rapid changes in the East German political system—which resulted in thousand of Trabants flooding through into West Germany—may well inspire new cars from Eisenach and Zwickau. These will probably be of West German design.

Rumania's car industry has been largely based on French designs. The Dacia was a Renault 12 with minor styling differences, while the Oltcit (shown here) was Citroen-derived: it used the 652-cc flat-twin or fours of 1129 or 1299 cc, in a three-door hatchback body styled after that of the Visa. Introduced in October 1981, the Oltcit was sold under the name Citroen Axel on the French market, where it undercut the 2CV by about 2000 francs. The top Oltcit had a five-speed gearbox, and an unusual feature for such a modestly priced car was the provision of disc brakes on all four wheels. This is a 1989 Czechoslovakian-registered Oltcit Club 11RL.

The early 1970s saw the peak of the American muscle cars. One of the most dramatic in appearance, as well as the fastest, was the 1970 Plymouth Superbird (opposite), the hottest model in the Road Runner range. It could be had with the 426 Hemi (6980 cc, 425 bhp, hemispherical combustion chambers) or 440 (7210 cc, 390 bhp) engine. The enormous rear wing was developed for NASCAR racing, in which Superbirds clocked 220 mph. Homologation for NASCAR events required at least 1,500 to be made, but in fact Plymouth built 1,920 Superbirds, all in the 1970 season. Dodge made an equivalent car in the Charger Superbee, and also the less dramatic-looking Charger R/T (above) which was offered with the 426 Hemi or 440 engine.

The United States of America

The 1970s were highly traumatic years for the United States. One of the two most powerful military nations in the world had to admit defeat by the North Vietnamese; fuel shortages threatened the cherished large American cars; and in 1980 they had to yield first place in the world's production league to Japan. Ever since well before 1914, Americans had always made more cars than any other country. Their 1970 figures were 6,550,203 passenger cars, more than double Japan's figure of 3,178,708. By 1980, America had dropped slightly to 6,375,506, while Japan had surged forward to 7,038,108.

Japan has maintained a lead every year since then, apart from 1986 when America made just 18,974 more. Even these figures do not tell the true story, for they include the large numbers of Japanese-designed cars made in the USA, one of the major trends of the 1980s. In 1989 America's best-selling car was the Honda Accord, the first time a car of foreign origin had taken this position. In December 1989 both Honda and Toyota sold more cars than Chrysler. Falling American sales were undoubtedly due to complacency, for the years of domination of their own market had made both management and workers uninterested in productivity and technical progress, preferring to put profits into higher salaries and fringe benefits.

The American industry was almost at its peak in 1970 (the record year was 1973, when 9.7 million cars were delivered), and also at a peak were the size and power of its products. On the one hand, engines were larger than they had been since before World War II, with Cadillac leading the field at 8.2 litres. Competition among the makers of muscle cars brought about outputs as high as 425 bhp (6980-cc hemi V8 fitted to Dodge Charger and Plymouth Roadrunner and Barracuda), and tuning firms could boost output considerably.

However, the muscle-car era was coming to an end, several years before the Arab oil embargo struck. The last year for the Dodge 426 hemi was 1971; for 1972, the Charger was powered by a larger but less powerful engine, the 440 (7210-cc) giving 330 bhp, while in 1973 the same engine gave only 280 bhp. The 440's last year was 1977, by which time Federal emission regulations had reduced it to 195 bhp.

The foreign influence on the US industry was already evident at the beginning of the 1970s, particularly in the Chrysler Corporation who marketed the Hillman Avenger as a Plymouth Cricket and the Mitsubishi Colt as a Dodge Colt. These were Chrysler's answer to the new sub-compacts made by Ford and GM, who could afford the vast development costs.

Ford Pinto and Chevrolet Vega

Ford's model was the Pinto, a two- or three-door coupé or station wagon powered by a choice of 4-cylinder engines, British-built 1.6-litre pushrod overhead-valve or German-built 2-litre single-overhead-camshaft. Chevrolet offered the home-grown Vega with similar body

Two other high-performance Americans of the early 1970s. The American Motors AMX (left) was a two-seater coupé, unusual at a time when contemporaries such as the Chargers and GTOs were all four- or five-seaters. It was created by shortening the Javelin bodyshell and reducing the wheelbase from 109 to 97 inches. The standard engine was a 4752-cc 225-bhp V8, but 5620-cc and 6390-cc units were options, the latter giving 315 bhp. Firmer suspension and bucket seats made the AMX the best-driving car American Motors ever built, but it did not find many customers—only 19,134 in the three seasons from 1968 to 1970.

Oldsmobile's 4-4-2, of which a 1971 coupé is shown (above), originated in a special line of the F-85 compact car in 1964. The name indicated four speeds, a four-barrel carburettor and dual exhausts. The largest and most powerful engine to go in the 4-4-2 was the 7456-cc 380-bhp V8 in the 1969 Hurst-equipped models. By 1971, the last year for the proper 4-4-2, output was down to a maximum of 340 bhp. Thereafter the name went on an option package, on mid-sized and compact Oldsmobiles, surviving until 1978.

Chevrolet's sub-compact of the early 1970s was the Vega (left). It used a new 4-cylinder 2.3-litre engine, with alloy block and single overhead camshaft driven by a cogged belt. Riding on a 97-inch wheelbase, it was made with three body styles: two-door sedan, three-door hatchback and three-door station wagon, besides a panel delivery van. A limited-edition 'hot hatch' was the Cosworth-Vega, with Cosworth-designed twin-overhead-camshaft head and fuel injection. Only 3,508 of these were sold, in 1975 and 1976, out of total Vega production of more than two million between 1971 and 1977.

Ford's Mustang underwent great changes in the first six years of the 1970s. The Mach 1 of 1970 (above) was a high-performance coupé which had debuted the previous year. Offered with engines from 5750 to 7013 cc (250–335 bhp), it was identified by a special grille and air scoop on the bonnet, while mechanically it had firmer suspension. The Mustang Sprint, introduced in mid-1972, could be had with competition suspension—but its chief distinction was its decor, with white paint and blue stripes edged in red, complementary colours being used in the interior.

By contrast, the 1974 Mustang 11, though still a four-seater coupé, was a totally different car, with wheelbase down from 109 to 96.2 inches. Here the only engine options were a 2294-cc four developing 88 bhp, and a 2780-cc 100-bhp V6. By 1976, when this notchback with Ghia trim (right) was made, a 4948-cc 134-bhp V8 was also available in the Mustang 11, but it never regained its muscle-car image.

In 1981 Ford's home-grown Pinto gave way to the European front-drive Escort, made originally as a three-door hatchback, which was joined for 1982 by a five-door hatchback and station wagon. There was also a Mercury version called the Lynx (left), shown here in 1987 form. Lynx prices were around $100–150 above those of the equivalent Escorts, and sales were less than half. The Lynx had its last year in 1987, being replaced in the Mercury line-up by the Mexican-built Tracer, a badge-engineered Mazda 323.

One of the biggest surprises of the 1980s was the inclusion of a Cadillac in the subcompact J-car range, which was also made overseas as the Vauxhall Cavalier, Opel Ascona and Holden Camira. Powered by a 1.8-litre 4-cylinder engine, Cadillac's version was called the Cimarron (above), a sister to the Buick Skyhawk, Chevrolet Cavalier, Oldsmobile Firenza and Pontiac J-2000. Although the Cimarron had some features to distinguish it from its humbler sisters, such as a sunshine roof and leather upholstery, its main distinction was its price ($12,131 compared with $7,297–7,931 for a Buick Skyhawk, which wasn't all that different). Capacity went up to 2 litres for 1983, and from mid-1985 there was an option of a 2.8-litre V6. However, none of this helped. The Cimarron's first year, 1982, was its best, with 25,968 sold; thereafter sales slid to a pathetic 6,454 in 1988. It did not feature in the 1989 programme.

only major foreign-made components were the Opel-built manual gearboxes. New for 1971, the Vega was offered in 'hot hatch' form in 1975/6 with a Cosworth-designed twin-overhead-camshaft head and electronic fuel injection. Unfortunately output was only 110 bhp in Federalized form, just 20 bhp more than the standard Vega, which compared poorly with the 140 bhp developed by the twin-cam Lotus engine used in the Jensen-Healey. Only 3,508 Cosworth Vegas were sold, out of total Vega production of nearly two million.

In 1976 the Vega was joined by Chevette, a smaller car which was an international design, made also in Brazil, Britain, Germany and Japan. It was 17 inches shorter than a Vega, which was dropped after 1977. International cars were now becoming commonplace in the US industry, for Chrysler began to make the European-designed Horizon in Detroit, selling it under the name Dodge Omni. This was a clear rival to the Chevette, and to the very successful VW Golf which was

styles to the Pinto, and a new 2.3-litre 4-cylinder engine with alloy block and cogged belt drive for its overhead camshaft.

The Vega was made in a new factory at Lordstown, Ohio, and the

One of the most unusual-looking cars of the 1970s was AMC's Pacer (right), launched for 1975 as 'the first wide small car'. Aimed at the Pinto/Vega market, the Pacer was designed to have a GM-built Wankel engine—but when this was cancelled, AMC used their 3.8- and 4.2-litre 6-cylinder engines, adding a 5-litre V8 from 1978. The hatchback body was almost as wide as it was long, and few liked its appearance. After sales of 72,158 in six seasons, the Pacer was dropped at the end of the 1980 model year.

sold in the US as the Rabbit, and for a time was made there as well (1978–1988).

Ford's competitor in this field was also an international car, the front-drive Escort. Designed jointly by the company's American, British and German branches as the 'Erika' project, it was made in all three countries with variations between the European and American models. Americans had fewer engine options, with only the 1.6-litre being available to start with, though a 2-litre diesel was offered from the 1984 to 1987 model years. Nothing approaching the sporty XR3 was offered, and indeed the only high-performance Fords for US customers were German-built Sierra XR4is and Scorpios, which were sold under the Merkur brand name from 1985 to 1989.

AMC joins forces with Renault

If the Big Three all had their foreign-originated models in production by the early 1980s, the much smaller American Motors Corporation had surrendered completely to foreign designs by the end of the decade. They had made various compact cars during the 1970s, including the 96-inch-wheelbase Gremlin (1970–78) and the extraordinary Pacer, launched in 1975 as 'The First Wide Small Car', with a short bonnet originally designed to hold a Wankel rotary engine, acres of glass and a hatchback body almost as wide as it was long.

Renault acquired a controlling interest in AMC in 1982 and, alongside the current AMC range of four-wheel-drive sedans and station wagons, put into production the Renault 9 under the name Alliance.

Renault's take-over of AMC in 1982 led to the manufacture of an Americanized Renault 9, under the name Alliance (above). Two- and four-door sedans were offered for 1983, joined by the Renault 11-based Encore hatchback for 1984 and a convertible for 1985. At $10,295 this was the lowest-priced convertible sold in America. Alliance/Encore sales began well, reaching over 208,000 in 1984. But poor quality control knocked them down to 150,000 in 1985, and only 35,000 in 1987.

This was followed a year later by the Encore, which was an Americanized Renault 11 hatchback–and in 1985 by an Alliance convertible, America's lowest-priced open car at $10,295. However, none

Ford's most successful car of the late 1980s was the mid-sized Taurus, made in sedan and station-wagon forms. Introduced in 1986, it was then powered by a transverse 2.5-litre four or a 2.8-litre V6. They were joined for 1988 by a 3.8-litre V5, and for 1989 by the SHO (Super High Output) twin-overhead-camshaft 24-valve V6. Developed with help from Yamaha, the SHO gave 220 bhp, and cars thus fitted had larger anti-roll bars and disc brakes all round. Mercury's version of the Taurus was the Sable, which had somewhat different styling and came only with V6 engines, though not the SHO. In 1989 the Taurus was the best-selling American-designed car, though just beaten to overall first place by the Honda Accord. Illustrated is a 1987 Taurus sedan.

Launched in the summer of 1987, the front-drive Pontiac Grand Prix coupé was a member of GM's W-car family, which included the Buick Regal, Chevrolet Lumina and Oldsmobile Cutlass Supreme. Fuel-injected V6 engines were offered: 2.8-litre and 3.1-litre normally aspirated, and a 205-bhp turbo version of the latter. With disc brakes all round, the Grand Prix was voted 1988 Car of the Year by Motor Trend Magazine.

of these sold well enough to keep AMC viable. After severe losses and shrinking sales, Renault decided to bow out, selling the company to Chrysler, who wanted to get their hands on the lucrative Jeep business, in 1987.

Thus the last American independent, whose ancestry could be traced back to the once-proud independents Hudson and Nash, was absorbed into the Big Three. Chrysler set up a new division, Jeep-Eagle, to make the Renault 25-based Premier sedan and the Renault 21-based Medaillon. The latter was imported from France, while the Premier was built in Canada.

Chrysler goes Japanese

Chrysler was the first American company to become involved with Japan, when they acquired a 15% stake in Mitsubishi in 1971. This rose to 24% in 1985, but fell back to 21.8% in 1988, when Mitsubishi issued new shares prior to becoming listed on the Tokyo Stock Exchange. In September 1989, Chrysler sold nearly half their holdings in order to raise much-needed capital, but they retained the important link in the Diamond Star project.

This was a joint venture with a factory at Normal, Illinois, where the same car was made for sale under the names Mitsubishi Eclipse and Plymouth Laser. It was launched in 1988 as a 2+2 coupé powered by a 1.8-litre 90-bhp single-overhead-camshaft engine in its entry-level form, with the option of a 135-bhp twin-cam 2-litre, or a 190-bhp turbo version. The chief differences between the Mitsubishi and Plymouth versions were that the former had front and rear spoilers, giving a better Cd figure of 0.29 compared with the Plymouth's 0.33. With a top speed of 140 mph, the Eclipse was excellent value at $17,000, whereas a VW Corrado cost 25% more. 1989 saw a 4×4 version, whose technology derived from the Galant saloon, called the Eagle Talon GSi or the Eclipse GSX, which was better able to transmit

The 1988 Chevrolet Turbo Sprint was actually a turbocharged Suzuki Swift GT (see page 27).

the 190 bhp to the road. Anticipated first-year production at Normal was 240,000 cars, not enough to meet domestic demand, let alone export markets.

GM and Isuzu

General Motors began their Japanese links when they acquired a 34.2% stake in Isuzu in 1971. This resulted in Isuzu's pick-up being sold in the USA as the Chevrolet LUV (Light Utility Vehicle). The next step was the T-car, made in Brazil and the US as the Chevette, and by Isuzu as the Gemini, under which name it was also sold in Australia by Holden. In the 1980s, GM developed more extensive ties with Japan, under which the Suzuki Swift and Isuzu Gemini were sold in the US as the Chevrolet Sprint and Spectrum, while a joint factory with Toyota called NUMMI (New United Motor Manufacturing Co. Inc.) was set up at Fremont, California, to make a Toyota Corolla-derived sedan or hatchback marketed as the Chevrolet Nova.

In 1989 these Japanese models were grouped under a new sub-division of Chevrolet, called Geo. The Sprint became the Geo Metro, the Spectrum the Geo Spectrum, and the Nova the Geo Prizm, while an additional model was the Geo Tracker (Suzuki Vitara). The Prizm was an American-made car, but the others were all imports, and contributed to the growing proportion of imported cars sold in the USA (3,197,000 in 1987, or 31.1% of the total).

Ford imports from Korea

Ford's imports came not from Japan but from Korea, where the Kia Festiva small 3-door hatchback was made for sale in the USA as the Ford Festiva. An almost identical design was made in Japan as the Mazda 121, Japanese-market cars being sourced from both Japan and Korea.

Ford also imported the Mazda 323-based Mercury Tracer from Mexico. Since 1986, Korea has also provided another 'American' car, the Pontiac Le Mans hatchback, which is an Opel Kadett made by

GM's Korean arm, the Daewoo Motor Company of Inchon.

All this international manufacture is a far cry from the situation in 1970, when a car badged as a Ford, Chevrolet or Plymouth was an all-American product. When considering the erosion of the US industry, one must also take into account the foreign plants operating in the States, whose products are counted as American cars, though some of the profits go to their parent companies.

As well as the joint NUMMI plant, Toyota now has a factory in Kentucky—whence Camrys were to be exported to Japan in 1990, to reduce Japan's trade imbalance with the US—and another in Canada. Hondas were made at Marysville, Ohio, from 1983; Mazdas at Flat Rock, Michigan, from 1985; and Nissans at Smyrna, Tennessee, from 1983. Volkswagen Golfs were made at New Scranton, Pennsylvania, from 1978.

The neo-classics

In 1964 Brooks Stevens offered a roadster styled after the 1928 Mercedes-Benz SS, powered by a Studebaker V8 engine. Christened Excalibur, his creation soon gained Chevrolet power as Studebaker went out of business. It offered, under the vintage appearance, such necessary modern comforts as synchromesh or automatic transmissions, power-assisted steering, and air conditioning on the closed models which followed in the 1970s. Excaliburs, which now include a four-door sedan, were still made in the late 1980s.

For a while they, and Glen Pray's 8/10ths-scale Cord 810 and full-size Auburn, were the only caterers to the nostalgia market. But the 1970s saw a sudden proliferation of what came to be known as the neo-classics.

These were of two kinds: more or less faithful replicas of interwar classics such as the Duesenberg J, and the more numerous examples—mostly two-door coupés designed in a parody of 1930s styling, with long bonnets, sweeping wings, sometimes dummy exhaust pipes and external spare wheels (or at any rate spare wheel covers), side- or rear-mounted or sometimes both.

One interpretation of the large-car theme in the 1980s was the conventional rear-drive 1984 Dodge Diplomat. All the Big Three manufacturers retained large rear-drive sedans for conservative customers who mistrusted front drive. These included taxi operators and the police, who made up the bulk of Diplomat buyers in the 1980s.

The nostalgia movement which swept America during the 1970s and 1980s resulted both in genuine replicas using modern power units, such as the Auburn (above), and in neo-classics which aped the 1930s style without reference to any particular make. The Auburn 853 boat-tailed speedster was a favourite of the replicar makers, at least three firms in the USA and one in Australia building it.

A typical neo-classic was the Clenet roadster (left). Made in Goleta, California, by French-born Alain Clenet, it used Lincoln Continental chassis and running gear, while the centre section of the body came from an MG Midget. It was produced from 1976 to 1982, a four-seater being added in 1981. At $83,000 it was by no means cheap—but better value than, for instance, the Buehrig which had a price tag of $130,000.

Power invariably came from a big V8, though as the years passed the available engines became smaller. So whereas a 1975 neo-classic might have boasted 7 litres and 350 bhp, its 1989 descendant had to manage on 5.2 litres and 150 bhp.

Excalibur of Milwaukee, Wisconsin, were the largest and oldest makers of neo-classics. Originally they had a fairly close resemblance to the Mercedes-Benz SSK, but during the 1970s their bodies grew more elaborate and the wheelbases longer. This Phacton rode on a 124-inch wheelbase and cost $71,865 in 1988.

Clenet, and Zimmer Golden Spirit

Neo-classics hailed mainly from Florida or California. Among the better-known examples were the Clenet built in Goleta, California, by French-born Alain Clenet, and the Florida-made Zimmer Golden Spirit, product of a company which had previously made mobile homes. The Clenet used Lincoln Continental running gear, with a two-seater body hand-formed from steel round the centre section of an MG Midget.

The Zimmer was a four-seater closed coupé with a Ford Mustang power train and Mustang centre section. Creating a Golden Spirit involved chain-sawing a Mustang monocoque in half, extending the forward part by at least three feet, and building a fibreglass 'period' body around the centre section, retaining the floor, doors, window glass and roof.

Internal fittings were very luxurious, with walnut dashboard, Italian leather upholstery and vases of Bohemian crystal. Priced at upwards of $90,000, the Golden Spirit seemed to sell quite well from its introduction in 1980, about 1,500 finding customers in eight years. But in 1989 the company was reported to be in trouble after launching

a modified Pontiac Fiero called the Quicksilver.

In fact, bankruptcies and changes of name and ownership were frequent among the makers of neo-classics, as they were in the kit-car world. The Clenet flourished from 1976 to 1982, and the design reappeared a year or two later as the Roaring Twenties. The Sceptre open two-seater was made at Goleta from 1978 to 1982, then went out of production to re-emerge as the Gatsby Griffin from San José, part of a range which included other neo-classics.

Most were two-door coupés or convertibles–but Knudsen from Omaha, Nebraska, offered a stretched limousine in classic style, as well as its Baroque cabriolet, both powered by a turbocharged 3.8-litre Buick V6. In a somewhat different category were the Stutzes, whose makers revived only the name of a classic model. Introduced in 1970, they had modern styling by Virgil Exner, bodies built by Padana in Italy, and Pontiac V8 engines.

Originally selling a two-door coupé for $22,500, the Stutz company later added a convertible, which by 1979 cost $107,000, and a limousine on a 172-inch wheelbase at $200,000.

The first Japanese company to show technical ingenuity was Mazda, who introduced a sports coupé powered by a Wankel rotary engine in 1967. By the mid-1970s, they had a complete range of Wankel-engined cars, though they played safe by offering a comparable range with the same bodies and conventional single-overhead-camshaft engines. This is a 1974 Wankel-powered RX-4 saloon. With a 1.8-litre conventional engine it would be a 929. Mazda dropped the large-scale production of Wankel engines because of their cost and heavier fuel consumption, but the RX-7 was still rotary-powered in 1989.

At least forty makes were announced between the mid-1970s and 1988, but with a high mortality rate, only 16 US neo-classics and one Canadian were listed in 1988. The breed was almost unknown in Europe, apart from the Clenet-like Dutch-built Desande, made from 1979 to 1984.

Japan

In his book *Cars of the Thirties and Forties*, the late Michael Sedgwick entitled a short chapter on the Japanese industry "The Hesitant Sunrise"; yet in a later work *Cars, 1946–1956*, his title was "Will the Sun Never Rise?" Twenty years later, the sun had not only risen but was threatening to scorch the rest of the world. In 1956 Japan made 32,000 passenger cars, of which just 46 were exported. By 1970 the figures had risen to 3,178,708 and 725,586, while in 1988 they made 8,198,400 of which 4,431,888 were exported–more than half. In addition, Japanese companies were manufacturing in some 10 foreign countries.

Renault by Hino, Austin by Nissan, Hillman by Isuzu

The other dramatic change over the past two decades, and one which may be more significant than sheer numbers, is that Japanese companies have taken the lead in several areas of technical development, whereas in 1970 they were largely content to copy European products. Indeed, in the 1950s and 1960s several firms made European cars under licence: Hino built Renault 4CVs; Nissan, Austin A40s; and Isuzu, Hillman Minxes.

By 1970 this had come to an end, but there was still little originality about most Japanese cars. Daihatsu's Compagno (the first Japanese car to be marketed in Britain, in 1966), Datsun's Sunny and Bluebird, Mazda's 1200, Toyota's Corona, were all conventional front-engine/rear-drive saloons with pushrod overhead-valve engines of no great output. Disc brakes were just appearing on the front wheels, and the Daihatsu, Datsun Sunny and Toyota still had semi-elliptic rear suspension.

The Datsun 240Z, best-selling sports car of its day, was a conventional design, though it did boast four valves per cylinder and, unusually for a Japanese car at that time, rack-and-pinion steering.

Mazda's Wankel engine

The only really innovative Japanese cars were the Mazdas, which used the Wankel rotary engine. Starting with the limited-production 110S sports coupé in 1967, Mazda installed rotary engines in the 1200 saloon to make the R100. During the early 1970s, they gradually extended the use of rotaries to most of their range, though hedging their bets by offering conventional engines in the same body-shells.

Thus the 818 coupés, saloons and estates had various sizes of single-overhead-camshaft engines, while the RX3 had the same range of bodies but was Wankel-powered. The same situation applied to the 929 and RX4 models. By 1978 Mazda had made more than a million Wankel-engined cars.

They still made the Wankel-engined RX7 sports car, but the design was discontinued for mass-produced cars, largely because financial problems at the end of the 1970s demanded a cheap-to-build, highly profitable car. This was the 323 hatchback which had a conventional single-overhead-camshaft engine.

The minicar–typically Japanese?

If we search for national characteristics, the one quintessentially Japanese car is the minicar below 550 cc. This type has long been favoured by tax concessions, and also by a law which allowed it to be parked by the pavement in large cities, which was forbidden to bigger cars. In the 1960s the capacity limit was 360 cc, and numerous manufacturers catered to this market–including Honda, whose 600-cc version was exported to Europe; Mazda with the R-360 coupé; and Daihatsu, Mitsubishi, Subaru and Suzuki. Two-cylinder air-cooled engines were featured, but the Honda had a single overhead camshaft, and by 1970 was offered with a three-speed automatic transmission.

During the next few years, minicars became more sophisticated. Typical of their progress was Suzuki, whose 1970 offering was the Fronte LC50 with rear-mounted 360-cc 3-cylinder 2-stroke engine. 1977 saw the 539-cc Cervo coupé (exported to Europe in 970-cc form) with front disc brakes, and two years later the engine was mounted

An attractive Japanese small car was the Suzuki Cervo, with rear-mounted 539-cc two-stroke or 547-cc single-overhead-camshaft four-stroke engine, front disc brakes and seating for two quite comfortably (four at a pinch). European market versions, as here, had 970-cc engines giving 76-mph top speed, and were called SC100. They were on the market from 1979 to 1982.

Another Japanese minicar which reached Europe was the Daihatsu Domino, or Cuore in its homeland. Only 126 inches long, it had limited luggage space, though it could seat four adults. Acceleration was leisurely, particularly in its 547-cc form, which was not exported. This 1982 UK-market model had 617 cc and 30 bhp. In 1986 it gave way to a four-door model with 846-cc 3-cylinder engine and front disc brakes.

transversely at the front driving the front wheels. A 543-cc four-stroke was an alternative to the 539-cc two-stroke. In 1983 the 543-cc engine was turbocharged to give 42 bhp.

By 1988 there were several sporting versions of the standard minis, such as Daihatsu's 47-bhp turbocharged Leeza, which had a more aerodynamic body than the regular Cuore (Domino in Europe); Subaru's turbocharged 55-bhp Rex, which also offered CVT automatic transmission and four-wheel drive; and Suzuki's twin-overhead-camshaft 12-valve Works, also with four-wheel drive.

Most exciting of all was the Mitsubishi Minica Dangan ZZ, whose 548-cc twin-overhead-camshaft turbocharged and intercooled 3-cylinder engine had five valves per cylinder, the first such layout to go into mass-production. Output was 64 bhp, which gave the little Dangan (126 inches overall length) a top speed of nearly 100 mph. Doubtless the engine could be developed further, but 64 bhp is the limit permitted by the Japanese government for cars under 550 cc.

None of the minicars is exported to Europe, but a solitary Dangan ZZ which came to England in 1989 captivated the rally driver Pentti

An example of the Japanese 'hot mini' which was introduced in late 1989. The Honda Today (left) had a 547-cc 3-cylinder engine with four valves per cylinder, and 44 bhp in fuel-injected form. Three transmissions were offered: four- or five-speed manual or three-speed automatic.

Nissan's nostalgia cars, the Pao and the S-Cargo (left), appeared as prototypes at the 1987 Tokyo Show, and were on sale about a year later. The Pao was deliberately austere, with only one dial (the speedometer) on the instrument panel, old-fashioned flick switches, simple hemp-like seat trim, and corrugated bonnet and side panels. Anachronistically modern features were the option of five-speed manual or three-speed automatic gearbox. Sixties enthusiasts certainly had to pay for the pleasure of owning a Pao. It cost the equivalent of £6,875 when a basic three-door Micra could be had for £2,835.

The S-Cargo (Escargot) evoked the spirit of the Citroen 2CV, though without that unconventional springing. It was powered by a 1487-cc engine, whereas the Pao made do with 985 cc. Both were limited-production cars: the Pao had a run of 10,000 like its predecessor the Be-1, while the S-Cargo was restricted to two years beween January 1989 and December 1990.

Airikkala and several hardened journalists who drove it. Minicars are big business in Japan; 1988 production was 156,108, and they are offered by all makers except the Big Two, Nissan and Toyota.

The latest variation on the theme is the mini sports car, as exemplified by two exhibits at the 1989 Tokyo Show. Suzuki's Cappucino had a 64-bhp 550-cc turbo engine and resembled a scaled-down Mazda MX-5, while Mazda's AZ-550 was a mid-engined gull-wing two-seater coupé. This was only a show car, but the Cappucino was destined for production.

Nostalgia minicars – remembering the early 1960s

Another uniquely Japanese vehicle was what could be called the nostalgia minicar. Whereas American nostalgia cars had acres of bonnet and recalled the 1930s, Japan's were mini-sized, though they used larger engines than the 550-cc cars, and recalled the early 1960s. Their development was sparked off by the great popularity of the British Leyland Mini, which was a cult car amongst smart young Japanese in the 1980s.

The first car to evoke the Mini's era was the Nissan BE-1, which appeared as a styling exercise at the 1985 Tokyo Show, and went into production the following year. Using running gear from the 1-litre Micra, the BE-1 has plain and simple styling reminiscent of the first Minis, with large round instruments incorporating black digits on white dials. It cost 50 % more than a Micra, yet Nissan sold about 400 per month.

It was succeeded in 1989 by the Pào, a continuation of the theme with even simpler seating and instrumentation–and by the S-Cargo, (Escargot), a curious little van with exaggeratedly rounded lines. The 1989 Tokyo Show saw the Figaro, a Micra-powered two-seater sports.

Japan threatens Jaguar and Mercedes

Not until the late 1980s did Japanese technology began to edge ahead of its foreign rivals–but its progress in the last few years has been remarkable, as has been its ability to challenge in every field. Of the three cars with four-wheel steering currently made, all are Japanese (Honda, Mazda, Mitsubishi). Much though Japan's small and medium-sized cars were respected, it was believed that Japan could never displace BMW, Mercedes-Benz or Jaguar from their positions in the quality field. Now the Nissan Infiniti and Toyota Lexus pose a real threat, particularly on the all-important American market.

Similarly, the Honda NS-X broke new ground in the sports-car field. Faster, more powerful and more expensive than any previous Japanese production car, this used a 24-valve V6 3-litre engine derived from that of the Legend, but with plenty of new engineering– including twin camshafts to each bank of cylinders. The engine was mounted transversely behind the driver, and drove the rear wheels by either a five-speed manual or four-speed automatic gearbox.

Among its sophisticated features were a traction-control system which reduced power to the rear wheels as soon as the brakes' anti-lock sensors detected variable slip. It also had anti-lock brakes with all four wheels having independent control systems. Despite high per-

'A mixture of high technology and proven sports-car design' was a good description of the Honda NS-X, powered by a transverse 3-litre 24-valve V6 mounted behind the driver. With 250 bhp, a top speed of 160–170 mph seemed likely, taking Honda into direct competiton with Porsche and Ferrari—hitherto unknown territory for a Japanese manufacturer. Yet unlike some supercars, the NS-X was easy to drive, with clutch and gear change as sweet as those of the Civic. Prototypes were running as early as 1984, and the NS-X made its debut at the beginning of 1989, with production starting in 1990.

formance (top speed of 170 mph), Honda's engineers aimed to make the NS-X suitable as a shopping car, thereby gaining an edge over the more overtly sporty European supercars.

Testers found the NS-X's gear change as easy as that of a Civic. Anticipated production was 5,000 per year–and at an estimated UK price of £37,000, this was probably too low to satisfy world-wide demand.

Tokyo Motor Show–a Mecca for new ideas

The inventiveness of Japanese technology was best seen at the biennial Tokyo Show, where during the 1980s every manufacturer exhibited several concept cars to test public reaction to new ideas. Some were very far-out, but a surprising number resulted in production cars a few years later.

This happened with Nissan's 'funny cars' Be-1, Pao and S-Cargo, and with Toyota's MR-2 mid-engined sports car. Nissan signalled to the world that it was aiming to challenge Mercedes and Jaguar when it exhibited the CUE-X luxury saloon at the 1985 show.

When the Infiniti appeared three and a half years later, it was not the same car by any means, but the theme had been established. Concepts such as Mazda's double-direction four-wheel-steering appeared on their show car, the MX-03, four years before it was seen on a production car.

Among the advanced concept cars at the 1989 show was Mit-subishi's HSR ll coupé, powered by 3-litre twin-turbo twin-intercooler

V6 engine, with four-wheel drive and steering, and aircraft-type computer controlled adjustment for the various spoilers, flaps and wings with which it was bedecked. Isuzu showed the 4200R mid-engined coupé, powered by a Lotus-designed 4.2-litre 350-bhp V8. Nissan had the Neo-X, a four-door saloon with hydraulic active suspension and Select-by-Wire five-speed automatic gearbox. It was an indication of what the Infiniti of the mid-1990s might be like.

Among innovative engines were a 3-litre supercharged 2-stroke from Toyota and a triple four or W12 from Mazda, with three banks of four cylinders, two overhead camshafts to each bank and 48 valves. As it was only four cylinders long, it could easily fit under the bonnet of a 626, and was a possible power unit for a future rival to the Lexus and Infiniti.

Subaru developed a 450-bhp flat-12 engine for the Jiotto Caspita gull-wing coupé, which might be used in a future Subaru luxury saloon. All these ideas were ahead of what was happening in European design studios, and were a measure of the threat which Japan will pose in every field in the 1990s.

The battle has just begun

In their marketing too, the Japanese are likely to present their most formidable challenge yet. In order to avoid the quota restrictions on imported cars, more Japanese companies are likely to set up European factories, following the lead of Nissan, Toyota and Honda. It was expected that by 1990, American factories would account for 20% of all Japanese car production.

In the early 1990s, Nissan aimed to build two cars outside Japan for every one built at home, their chief foreign plants being in Britain, the United States, Spain, Mexico and Australia. During the same period, Honda hoped to sell 300,000 cars annually in Europe, half of which would come from their British plant at Swindon and the Rover factory at Longbridge.

Japan's involvement with Korea was set to grow significantly, with that country making a growing proportion of the smaller cars. There were also plans for Daihatsu to cooperate with FSO in Poland, supplying technology for small diesel engines, while Suzuki was planning to build Altos in Hungary.

Japan had an important presence in Australia. Daihatsu and Suzuki were supplying or issuing licences for the manufacture of most of China's light vans. Surely it is only a matter of time before they make cars there as well. By the end of the 1980s, the sun had not only fully risen, but its rays were extending into practically every corner of the earth.

A world of cars

The 1980s saw car production extend well beyond the traditional centres of Europe, America and Japan. There had been industries in Brazil and Argentina since the 1950s, while Australia had a history of assembly and manufacture dating back to before World War I. Korea, Taiwan and Malaysia, on the other hand, were never thought of as car-making countries until quite recently.

Korea

Korea has made the most significant growth, output rising from 17,750 passenger cars in 1973 to 866,000 in 1988. Their leading company was Hyundai, a branch of a vast industrial corporation mainly involved in shipbuilding and civil engineering.

Hyundai began by assembling British Ford cars and trucks in 1968, turning to manufacture seven years later with the Pony, a conventional four-door saloon styled by Ital Design and powered by a 1238-cc Mitsubishi engine. The organization of the factory, and coordination of the international chain of design and production, was the work of the Englishman George Turnbull, formerly managing director of the Austin-Morris Division of British Leyland.

The simple, old-fashioned Pony with rear-wheel drive and semi-elliptic rear suspension sold well on the strength of its low price. Canada was a significant export market, and within two years of the Pony's arrival there, Hyundai became the best-selling Canadian import. 1985 saw a more modern Pony with transverse Mitsubishi engines and front drive. Following international trends, Hyundai

The 1989 introduction of Hyundai's front-drive Sonata was a major move up-market for the Korean manufacturer. Three engines from 1.8 to 2.4 litres, and two levels of trim, gave a six-model range, with the choice of five-speed manual or four-speed automatic gearboxes. A competitor for the Ford Sierra Sapphire 2.0i or Vauxhall Carlton 1.8i, the 2-litre Sonata undercut both, though it could not match their performance.

Malaysia entered the ranks of the world's motor manufacturers in 1985, with the Mitsubishi-based Proton Saga saloons and hatchbacks. Exports to Europe began in 1988—and in 1989 Great Britain was the largest export market, taking 77%, while Ireland was second and New Zealand third. This is a 1989 1.5 SE Aeroback, as Proton called their hatchbacks.

offered a hatchback version as well, known as the Sonnet. They also extended their market coverage with the Stellar, a conventional rear-drive car with Ford Cortina IV chassis engineering and 1597-cc Mitsubishi engine. Styling was again by Ital Design.

During the 1980s, Hyundai production shot up, from 91,000 in 1982 to 226,000 in 1985. They confidently expected to reach the million mark in 1990. Their first overseas plant, in Canada, opened in 1989, and some sources were predicting a European Hyundai factory by the mid-1990s. As production grew, so did the range and quality.

New for 1989 was the Sonata, a medium-sized front-drive car with engines of 1796, 1997 or 2351 cc, the latter with fuel injection and the option of a catalytic converter. A competitor in the Ford Sierra class, but at a lower price, the well-equipped Sonata together with a new two-door 2+2 coupé for 1990 marked a further step by Hyundai towards a broad international range.

Korea's second largest car company was Daewoo, which is 50% owned by General Motors, and built various GM products under licence. These included the Maepsi-Na (Isuzu Gemini), Le Mans (Opel Kadett, sold in the US as the Pontiac Le Mans), Royale (Opel Rekord) and Royale Super Salon (Opel Senator). For 1990 Daewoo were planning a new saloon to rival Hyundai's Sonata, and one which would owe less to Opel than previous products, having Bertone styling. Daewoo made only 55,000 cars in 1986, but anticipated an output of 600,000 by 1991. This would clearly necessitate a considerable export drive, but given Hyundai's success there is no reason why they should not achieve it.

K.I.A. was set up in 1977 as a joint venture by Mazda and Ford to make a range of Mazdas. In 1985 appeared a small three-door hatchback with 1138-cc or 1324-cc transverse engines driving the front

wheels. Known on the local market as the Kia Pride, and exported to the USA as the Ford Festiva, it was very similar to the Mazda 121. In fact some of the Japanese market Mazda 121s were made by Kia.

In 1989 Kia added two larger models to its range, the Mazda 323-based Capital and the 626-based Concord. Kia's production target for 1991 was 900,000 cars. If this is realized, and added to Daewoo's 600,000 and Hyundai's million plus, it will put Korea's industry ahead of Great Britain's. Truly Korea may well become a second Japan on the world scene.

Malaysia

A younger motor industry is that of Malaysia where the first cars came off the line in 1985. Based on the Mitsubishi Lancer, the Proton Saga was offered as a saloon or hatchback, with a choice of 1.3- or 1.5-litre engines. Bodies were styled and made in Selangor, and local content accounted initially for 42% of the ex-factory value of the car, a proportion which rose in succeeding years.

Protons were well-equipped for their price, top-of-the-range models featuring power steering, central locking, electrically operated

The Shanghai SH-760A was the only native Chinese car to be built in any numbers—and even so, production ran at no more than 3,000 per year. A 1960s design, it had a 2.2-litre pushrod overhead-valve 6-cylinder engine, coil-and-wishbone front suspension with semi-elliptics at the rear. Most Shanghais were used as taxis or for official transport.

windows and door mirrors as standard. Exports to Europe started in 1988, and production rose from 24,200 in 1987 to an estimated 80,000 in 1989.

Taiwan

Taiwan's cars were also Japanese-based. The Yue Loong company of Taipei had links with Nissan dating back to 1958. In the 1970s they made variants of the Datsun Bluebird and Cedric, joined in 1974 by the Violet and in 1977 by the Sunny. Their offering for the late 1980s was the 101 or Feeling, still Nissan-based but with more individual styling. Its power train was derived from that of the previous generation's Nissan Stanza, with engines of 1.6 and 1.8 litres.

Taiwan's other car maker, Ford Lio Ho, dated from 1986 when they began to make a Mazda 323-based car called the Tracer. This was exported to Canada, where it was sold under the name Ford Mercury. Taiwan's motor industry was small compared with that of Korea; 1987 production was 99,640, of which rather more than half were Yue Loongs.

China

Mainland China moved from very small production of local designs to a growing involvement with foreign countries, of which France, Germany, the United States and Japan were the most prominent. Car ownership was miniscule, about one per 10,000 of the population, compared with one per 1.72 in the United States, one per 2.75 in Great Britain, one per 2.16 in West Germany and one per 21 in the Soviet Union.

In 1988, 80% of China's 3.5 million road vehicles were trucks, and cars did not account for more than 100,000, of which over 80,000 were taxis or government-owned. Even Zhav Sheng, senior engineer of

China's motor industry, does not own a car. Native offerings in the 1970s were restricted to two 'makes', Shanghai and Hong-Ki, together with the Jeep-like Beijing BJ-212.

The Shanghai was a Cortina-sized four-door saloon of 1960s appearance, powered by a 90-bhp 2.2-litre pushrod overhead-valve engine. Made since 1965 with little change, it was supplemented in the 1980s by a licence-built Volkswagen Santana. Production of this started in 1984, and in 1988 was running at 60 cars per day. By 1990 it was expected to rise to 250 per day. Made in an adjoining factory to the Shanghai, the Santana was set to replace the old-fashioned Chinese design (present production 5,000 per year) by the early 1990s. SVW (Shanghai Volkswagen Automotive Company Ltd) hoped to begin Santana exports in 1992.

The Passat Variant was made in another factory in Shanghai, as was the Audi 100, though this was transferred to Changchun in 1989. The Golf was also expected to enter production at Changchun, using dies from the former American VW factory. The Golf's rival will be the Citroen AX to be made at Wuhan.

Other foreign designs made in China included the Peugeot 504 pick-up and 505 estate car (5,000 made in 1988) and various models of Jeep (4,000 in 1988). These were well below the theoretical figures of 30–60,000 for Jeep and 30,000 for Peugeot, but shortages of foreign currency for the purchase of components have frequently interrupted production.

However, as the proportion of Chinese-made components rises, so should production. Although Japanese companies have been involved in the manufacture of vans and minibuses, they have not so far played much part in car development, apart from the use of the 993-cc 3-cylinder Daihatsu engine in the Zhonghua fibreglass-bodied car and pick-up, and licence manufacture of the Daihatsu Charade under the name Xiali. The only other native Chinese design was the Hong-Ki (see Chapter 2), made in extremely limited numbers.

A 36-year-old design still produced in India was the Hindustan Ambassador, based on the 1954 Morris Oxford. Apart from small styling changes, the Hindustan differed from the Morris mainly in using overhead-valve engines, including a diesel.

India

India has long been renowned for making obsolete European designs, and this pattern has continued during the last two decades. The oldest model was the Hindustan Ambassador, introduced in 1959, whose body was a 1954-design Morris Oxford, though it differed from the Morris in having an overhead-valve engine currently available in 1489-cc and 1760-cc versions, as well as a 2-litre diesel. It was still made in 1989, but six years earlier Hindustan advanced firmly into the late 1960s with the Contessa. This used the body dies of the FD Series Vauxhall Victor with the same engine options as the Ambassador. Hindustan also made the Jeep-like Trekker from 1977. The total production of all vehicles from this factory was 24,200 in 1984.

In 1973 there was an attempt to make an Indian-designed people's car, the Maruti−named after a sacred monkey. It had a rear-mounted 676-cc 2-cylinder air-cooled engine and a four-seater monocoque saloon body. Sanjay Gandhi, son of the then Prime Minister, Indira Gandhi, took a keen interest in the Maruti, and there were plans to make up to 60,000 cars per year.

However, it never got beyond the prototype stage, probably because it was an old-fashioned design unsuitable even for the undemanding Indian market. The company remained in business, though, and after the Government relaxed rules against imported engines in 1980, they began to make the Suzuki Fronte four-door saloon under the name Maruti 800. This was still made in 1989, though Suzuki had given up its manufacture in Japan.

With about 70,000 units made in 1988, it was the largest Indian make, well ahead of Mahindra who made Jeep CJs (c. 30,000) and Hindustan (c. 25,000). Other foreign-based Indian cars of the 1980s included the Premier Padmini (Fiat 1100) and 118E (Fiat 124 with Nissan Cherry engine), the Standard Gazel (Triumph Herald), which gave way to another Standard (Rover SD1 with 2-litre 4-cylinder engine), and the Sipani Dolphin (Reliant Kitten).

Australia

The Australian motor industry has undergone great changes since 1970, largely due to joint developments with Japan. Until 1980 the American Big Three dominated, led by GM's Holden division, and followed by Ford Motor Company of Australia and Chrysler Australia Ltd. The most individual make was Holden, who had been making 'Australian Cars for Australian People' since 1948. Their 1970 offerings ranged from the Vauxhall Viva-based Torana to big sedans with 4.1- or 5-litre V8 engines.

From 1968 to 1976 they had their own equivalent of the American muscle cars, the Monaro coupé powered by a 7.4-litre Chevrolet engine. The smaller V8s were Australian-designed. But in 1979 the Torana was dropped, its place at the bottom of the range having been taken by the Gemini. This was the Isuzu version of the international GM T-car, sold in Britain and the USA as the Chevette.

The second non-Australian Holden was the Commodore, based on the Opel of the same name, though with some styling differences and a wide range of engines from a 1.9-litre four to a 4.1-litre V8. It quickly became Australia's best-selling car until displaced by the Ford Falcon in 1982. That was the year in which Holden lost its position as Australia's best-selling make to Ford, a severe blow to the GM company who had thought of themselves as the undisputed leaders since 1950.

Australian Fords were similar to their American counterparts until 1972, when locally styled versions of the compact Falcon and full-size Fairlane were made. In 1979 the Falcons and Fairmonts resembled European Granadas. They were made with 6- and 8-cylinder engines until 1982 when the V8s were dropped, leaving Holden in command of the large-car market. They affirmed their faith in this by bringing out a new Statesman in 1983, with 5-litre V8 engine.

Still, Ford remained ahead in the sales league, and have stayed there up to 1989. During the 1980s, they widened their range by taking advantage of Ford's international links with Mazda. The Ford Laser was based on the Mazda 323 and the Telstar on the 626.

Meanwhile, Chrysler Australia had given up manufacture of the American-style Valiant, and their factory was given over to making various Mitsubishi models. These included the Colt Galant, which was marketed in Britain under the name Lonsdale in 1983–4, in order to circumvent the import quotas for Japanese cars. However, this rather old-fashioned car, similar to the obsolete Cortina, did not succeed on the UK market, and only 583 were sold.

Holden's version of the intrnational J-car was the Camira, seen here in 1984 form. It was also made as a station wagon, whose panels were exported to Britain for the Vauxhall Cavalier station wagon. Some engines for British, German and South African-built J-cars came from Holden. And all Opel engines for the Swedish market were Holden-built, as Swedish and Australian emission regulations were similar.

Complicated links with Japan

Australian links with Japan have become formidably complicated in the late 1980s. As well as the Ford/Mazda and Chrysler/Mitsubishi tie-ups, Nissan and Toyota had their own plants in Australia, establishing connections with Ford and Holden respectively. Because of the limited domestic market (about 450,000 annually), model-sharing became inevitable, and government senator John Button suggested a maximum of seven models throughout the industry.

Thus, in 1989, Holden and Toyota announced a new range of three models, carrying six badges: the Holden Nova/Toyota Corolla, Holden Apollo/Toyota Camry, and Holden Commodore/Toyota Lexcen. The latter used an American-sourced General Motors 3.8-litre V6 engine mounted longitudinally and driving the rear wheels, whereas in its American applications–in cars such as the Buick Le Sabre and Electra, or Oldsmobile Cutlass Ciera–the engine was mounted transversely and drove the front wheels.

The body was based on that of the Opel Omega, and the cars featured disc brakes all round. Because it was GM-derived, there was no equivalent in the Japanese Toyota range, unlike the smaller Holden/Toyotas. Nor was the 4.9-litre V8 engine used in the most powerful Commodore available in the Lexcen.

Under the Button Plan (recalling pre-war Germany's Schell Plan), Nissan Australia made the mid-size front-drive Pintara, which was

Top of the 1989 Holden range was the new VN series Commodore, with its luxury-equipped version the Calais (above). The standard engine was a 3.8-litre V6, whose castings came from the USA, with machining and assembly in Australia. An option was a 5-litre 221-bhp V8. Under the Button Plan for sharing designs, the Commodore body and V6 engine were also used by Toyota for their Lexcen, though this was not available with the V8 engine.

also badged as a Ford Telstar, thus ousting the Mazda 626 which had formerly carried this name. Whereas Nissan once made the Pulsar which was badged by Holden as an Astra, under the new plan they were likely to ask for the Mazda-based Laser to be rebadged as a Pulsar.

If they retain the 1.8-litre engine from the former Pulsar, the new one will be a Mazda 323 built in Australia under Nissan control and powered by a Holden engine. No wonder the ordinary buyer does not know what nationality his car is! Ford also made the Laser-based Capri open sports car for export to the US and other world markets, described in Chapter 3.

Introduced in 1982, the face-lifted Australian Ford Falcon XE was its country's best-selling car the following year. It was available with 6-cylinder and V8 engines from 3.3 to 4.9 litres. The last V8 Falcon was delivered in November 1982. This is a 1986 Falcon S-Pack, with 4.1-litre 6-cylinder engine and a top speed of 115 mph.

Two smaller Fords were built for 1986, both based on Japanese designs. The Laser was a Mazda 323, and the Telstar (above) a Mazda 626. Launched in 1980 and 1983 respectively, they were still part of the Ford range in 1989. The Telstar illustrated is a Ghia-trimmed TX-5 model with alloy sports wheels.

Apart from the Big Three, Australia's motor industry consisted of a number of very small firms making sports cars, usually in kit form. One of the best-known was the Bolwell Nagari, a fibreglass-bodied Ford V8-powered sports car in coupé or open form, of which about 120 were made between 1969 and 1974. Some were supplied as kits.

Campbell Bolwell of Mordialloc, Victoria, tried again in 1979 with the mid-engined VW-powered Ikari, but only a dozen kits were made, and the jigs were then sold to Greece. From 1970 to 1976, British-born Peter Pellandine offered the Pellandini gull-wing coupé using BMC Mini/1100 components, and built an experimental steam car with a 40-bhp double-acting 2-cylinder engine. The condenser doubled as a wing above the rear end. Other marginal ventures included the Corvette-like Holden-powered Perentti of 1982, an Austin Healey 3000 replica called the Pandarus, and the D.R.B. 2+2 coupé sold in kit form to take VW or Mazda rotary engines.

South Africa

The South African scene was similar to Australia's, with replacement of European and American cars by Japanese ones on an even greater scale. In 1970 General Motors, Ford and BMW all had substantial presences in South Africa. GM cars wers sold under two brand names–Chevrolet for the larger models, and Ranger.

Billed as 'South Africa's Own Car', this was a real international cocktail, with Opel Rekord bodyshell, a choice of Chevrolet 2120-cc or 2570-cc engines, Vauxhall Victor front suspension and optional auto-

matic transmission from Holden. It was made until 1973, after which all GM South Africa products wore Chevrolet badges, though a Belgian-assembled Ranger with Opel engines survived until 1976. The larger South African Chevrolets, the Kommando, Constantia and De Ville sedans were essentially Holdens with 6- or 8-cylinder engines. After 1982 the Chevrolet name was dropped, and GM South Africa made Opel-derived models.

BMW made a hybrid car from 1968 to 1975. This used the body-shell of the defunct Glas 1700 with BMW 1600 or 1800 engines. After 1975, they made various models of German BMW including the 5 and 7 Series, but withdrew from South Africa in 1988. Ford had few specifically South African models, though there were regional variations and one indigenous variant was the Sierra XR8, a high-performance five-door hatchback powered by a 4.9-litre V8 engine.

Other models included Escorts, Cortinas and Granadas, the latter made into 1985, after it had been dropped from the European Ford ranges. The South African Ford factory was also the source of Sierra pick-ups marketed in Europe. Volkswagen also made a variety of cars in their South African factories: Beetles as well as Golfs, Jettas and Passats. As with Ford, they tended to continue older designs, such as the square-fronted Golf and Jetta, after they had been superseded in Germany.

In numbers, the leading manufacturer by the late 1980s was Toyota, whose Corolla and Cressida accounted for about 25% of the 200,000 cars manufactured in the Republic in 1987. Second was Volkswagen with 20%, while other important Japanese manufacturers

included Nissan, Honda and Mazda. These seemed set to take a growing proportion of the market in the early 1990s.

Latin America: Brazil

Although virtually unknown outside their own territories, the Latin American countries had extensive and varied motor industries. The leading countries, as one would expect, were the two largest, Argentina and Brazil. In the main, their factories turned out licence-built versions of European or American cars, but there were some curious international cocktails such as the Brazilian Ford Corcel, which used Renault 12 suspension with styling which could be described as Renault 12 modified by Ford, and Ford engines of 1289 or 1400 cc. It was made from 1969 to 1987.

There was also a hatchback version known as the Del Rey, still current in 1989, alongside the Escort 1600 and various breaks and pickups. In 1988 Ford do Brasil and Volkswagen do Brasil formed a joint company, Autolatina, the first fruit of which was the adoption of the Golf 1800 engine in the Escort XR3. A Ford-powered Polo was likely to follow. VW do Brasil themselves made several distinctive models, including the SP fastback GT coupé with 1600 engine (introduced in 1971), the 1600-based Brasilia estate car (new for 1973), and the Gol of 1980.

This curious blend of old and new had a front-mounted Beetle engine driving the front wheels, combined with a hatchback body on

the lines of the Golf–though of individual style. There was also a notchback version called the Voyage. From 1987 the Gol was sold on the US market under the name Fox. The Brasilia was dropped in 1983, and the last Beetle came off the São Paulo production lines in 1986, leaving Mexico as the only country making the famous fifty-year-old design.

VW do Brasil was the country's biggest car maker and one of the largest employers of labour. Second was Ford, followed by General Motors and Fiat. GM built various Opel/Chevrolet hybrids in the 1970s, but were most famous for the Chevette which was in fact launched in Brazil before any other markets. It was still made in 1989, together with the Opel-based Monza sedan and convertible, and the larger rear-drive Opala, Commodoro and Diplomata with engines up to a 4.1-litre 6-cylinder.

Fiat Automoveis SA was set up in 1976, making the 127-derived 147, using a 1049-cc overhead-camshaft engine, joined by a 1.3-litre version in 1980. They also took over manufacture of the Brazilian-built Alfa Romeo 2300, formerly known as the FNM. From 1978 to 1988 it was sold under the name Fiat Alfa Romeo Ti-4, joining the two famous names several years before the companies were merged in

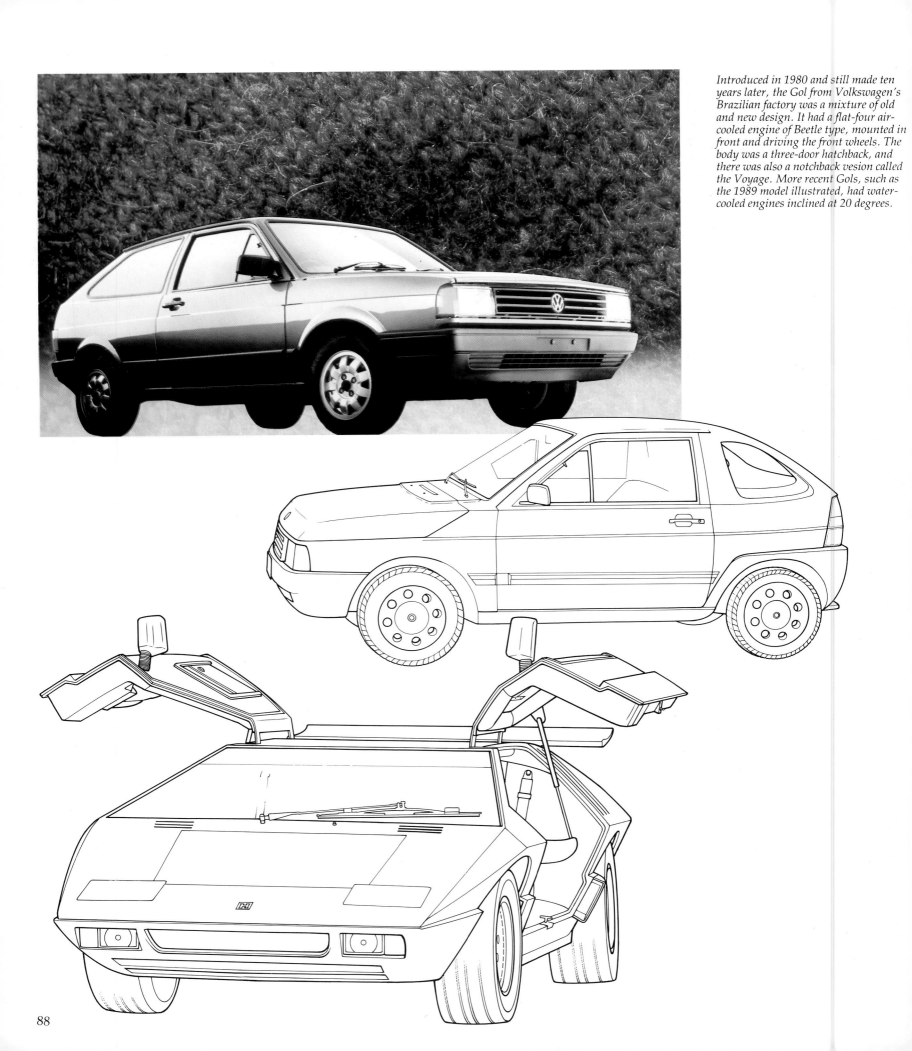

Introduced in 1980 and still made ten years later, the Gol from Volkswagen's Brazilian factory was a mixture of old and new design. It had a flat-four air-cooled engine of Beetle type, mounted in front and driving the front wheels. The body was a three-door hatchback, and there was also a notchback vesion called the Voyage. More recent Gols, such as the 1989 model illustrated, had water-cooled engines inclined at 20 degrees.

Italy. More recent Brazilian Fiats have included the Uno and booted and estate versions called Premio and Elba. In 1988 these began to be sold on the Italian market as the Duna and Duna Weekend, yet another example of today's global car industry.

Apart from the four major multi-national companies, Brazil had a large number of smaller car makers. Longest-established was the Puma, a VW-powered coupé and convertible whose lines were a cross between a Porsche 911 and an Alpine Renault. Made from 1969, it was joined by a Chevrolet-powered front-engined GT coupé in 1973. Production of both models lasted up to the mid-1980s when it was suspended, only to be revived by new owners in 1988.

The Puma was the only small Brazilian make to be exported, being offered on the Swiss market and exhibited at the 1973 London Racing Car Show – although how many were sold in either Britain or Switzerland is uncertain. Of the other small makes, probably the most distinctive was the Gurgel. Made since 1966, it started life as a buggy-like open off-road four-seater powered by a rear-mounted VW Beetle engine. Closed models were added in the 1970s, together with the Itaipuru electric car, the Carajas 4×4 with water-cooled front-mounted VW 1600 engine, and two versions of a small town car: the three-seater XEF powered by a rear-mounted VW Beetle engine, and the 280M with 800-cc horizontal-twin engine at the front. The XEF was only made for a few years from 1983, but the 280M was new in 1988.

Other Brazilian marginal companies were too numerous to mention individually. They included several replicars of Ford Thunderbird, Jaguar XK120, Mercedes-Benz 280SL and MG TD, and various GT coupés such as the VW-powered Adamo CRX 1800 and Miura Saga, and the Farus coupé and cabriolet which was offered with VW, Fiat or Chevrolet power.

Life was not easy for these little companies. One of the smallest, Hofstetter, who made a turbocharged VW Santana 1800-powered gull-wing coupé, admitted in their 1989 catalogue that production was restricted by the shortage of components, the Brazilian economy and shifting value of the cruzeiro/dollar exchange rate. They made only four cars in 1988.

A newcomer in 1988 was the P.A.G., a small two-door saloon on a VW Saviero pick-up base, with fibreglass body and choice of VW 1600 or 1800 engines. Another field in which Brazil was active was in 4×4 cross-country vehicles. These ranged from the little VW 1600-powered Dacunha Jeg to the Chevrolet- or Ford-powered Envemo and S.R., both four-seater crew-cabbed pickups. All Brazilian cars were equipped to run on alcohol fuel as an alternative to petrol.

Argentina

The Argentine industry was smaller, but also included several local variations of multi-national designs. Ford Argentina, established in 1962, made American-type Fairlanes and Falcons, the latter still current in 1988, more than 20 years after it was discontinued in the USA. More recent Ford products have included the Taunus (1975–1984) and the current Escort and Sierra.

Renault Argentina made the Torino, which was derived from a 1960s American Motors design, with 3- or 3.8-litre 6-cylinder engines and Pininfarina-styled bodywork from 1968 to 1983. They have also made various French Renaults, including the 4, 11, 12, 18 and Fuego – and the Jeep, inherited from their acquisition of IKA, the Argentine branch of Kaiser Industries which also brought them the Torino.

Other Argentine makes were the Sevel, which fused Fiat and Peugeot interests from 1980, offering the former's 600, 125, 128, 147 (Brazilian) and Regata, and the latter's 504 and 505; and VW Argen-

tina, which made the Gacel based on the Brazilian VW Voyage and, for a while, the Hillman Avenger. Marginal firms have been much fewer in Argentina than in Brazil. But they included the Eniak, a 1930s-style sports car offered with VW or Ford Falcon power, and the Crespi, a Renault 12-powered front-drive GT coupé.

Mexico

Of the other Latin American countries, the only one to have a significant industry was Mexico, where branches of Ford, GM, Chrysler, Nissan and Volkswagen flourished. The Ford factory at Hermosillo made a version of the Mazda 323 which was sold in the USA as the Mercury Tracer. A similar car was made in Taiwan for the Canadian market.

VW's Mexican plant is famous as the only one where the Beetle was still made in 1989. In 1989, it was also making the Golf, Jetta and Santana, the latter renamed the Corsar.

Renault and GM had branches in Columbia during the 1980s. The former made the 9 and 18, while the GM factory made the Chevrolet San Remo, based on the Opel Kadett. Ecuador had a short-lived make, the Aymesa, built by Autos y Maquinas de Ecuador SA of Quito. It was a three-door hatchback powered by a Brazilian Chevrolet 1.4-litre engine, and lasted only from 1981 to about 1986. The sole representative from Uruguay was the Halcon, a Ford Falcon-powered 1930s-style sports car, made to order by Montevideo's Rolls-Royce and Rover importer. Introduced in 1978, it was only built for a few years.

"13 YEARS AGO I BOUGHT THIS VOLVO BECAUSE IT WAS ADVERTISED AS THE 11 YEAR CAR."

— William Stiles, Bronx, New York

13 years ago, William Stiles, an expert in American Indian history and artifacts, discovered the treasure you see here: a 1966 Volvo.

He bought it because ads of the time said Volvos were so durable they lasted an average of 11 years in Sweden.

As Mr. Stiles recalls: "One ad said that a Volvo was so tough, you could 'Drive it like you hate it.' I did exactly that. In my field work I've driven this car 295,000 hard miles, much of it through former Indian territory. It's held up even better than promised. Driving it like I hated it made me love it."

Expressions of love are not uncommon among Volvo owners. In fact, 9 out of 10 people who have bought new Volvos are happy.

So if you're unhappy with your current car, do what Mr. Stiles once did after reading one of our ads. Buy one of our cars.

VOLVO

A car you can believe in.

4

CARS OF THE NINETIES
by Bengt Ason Holm

When the Eighties ended our society had begun to suffer from a world wide recession. Interest rates rose and borrowing money became expensive and the market for expensive classics and supercars almost died overnight.

One good example is the Jaguar XJ220 affair. When this supercar was introduced at the 1988 British Motor Show, Jaguar had no intention of building the car but 1,500 orders made Sir John Egan change his mind. The XJ220 got a price tag of £361,100 which was about twice the price of the newly introduced Ferrari F40 and the deposit for the XJ220 was £50,000.

When the updated XJ220 finally, in 1991, was unveiled in Tokyo the world was in the midst of the financial crisis and many customers were unable to fulfill their contracts.

The crisis was also to be seen in the total world production of ordinary cars. In 1990 there was an all time high with 36,185,000 produced cars. Then production slowly began to decrease to as low as 33,611,000 in 1993. Not until 1995 the number of produced cars passed the 1990 record.

In 1990 the leading companies were General Motors (7.5 m), Ford (5.9 m) and Toyota (3.1 m). Ten years later these three companies still hold their respectively positions.

What happened in the Nineties?

When Nick Georgano wrote the "Cars of the Seventies and Eighties" in the end of 1989 he finished the book with an epilogue entitled The Way Ahead. In that chapter he told the readers about what he thought about the future of the car.

Today, when we are sitting with the results in our hand, it's easy to see that most of his predictions were right, other wasn't.

One of the predictions was that we were going to see a wider range of cars, both makes and models. That's true because today we can find car manufacturers all over the world. Not only in Europe, Japan and USA but all over the world. Some of the small ones are still independent but most of the companies are, in one way or another, owned by some of the giants.

Regarding the model range we have witnessed an invasion of different models from the manufacturers. In 1988 for example, BMW and Audi had 26 respectively 33 different versions of their models. In 1999 this figures were 52 respectively 86.

The globalization

In 1964 there were 52 economical independent car manufacturers, a figure which in 1999 had decreased to 13 groups of companies which produced about different 2,000 models. Between 1998 and 2000 Ford bought Volvo, Daimler-Benz and Chrysler joined forces, Renault bought 37% in Nissan and the whole of Rumanian Dacia. General Motors increased their shares in Isuzu and Suzuki, Toyota got 51% of the shares in Daihatsu and Volkswagen bought Bentley, Bugatti, Lamborghini and Rolls-Royce. And in the beginning of the year 2000 there were many speculations about possible marriages in the near future. Was the French PSA group (Peugeot & Citroën) going to be sold to Ford or Chrysler? Was Fiat going to sell their car division, who was going to help BMW and was Toyota going to take over General Motors?

The technical evolution

The most asked question in the 90s was if the electric car was going to have a breakthrough. The answer is no. Most manufacturers experimented with different

1991 BMW E1. 200 kg of batteries and a top speed of 120 km/h made this little car something of a racer and the radius of action was 250 km.

This is Volvo's hybrid car, the ECC, from 1992. It was created in California at the Volvo Monitoring & Concept Center. It had both a gas turbine with supercharger and an electric engine. The lines of the ECC later came back in the Volvo S80, especially the curious rear-end.

solutions and some of them had dutifully an electric model in their model range. But they didn't do too much to encourage private people to buy them. The majority of electric cars were utility vehicles sold to local administrations.

One serious attempt was done by BMW when they in 1991 presented the BMW E1. Despite 200 kg of batteries the car had a very good top speed of 120 km/h and a 250 km (156 miles) radius of action. The output of the engine was 44 bhp and the chassis was made of aluminum. The body consisted of recyclable plastics.

Because of problems with the efficiency of the batteries many companies experimented with hybrid cars which could be driven with either electricity or petrol. Among them were Volvo ECC and Volkswagen Chico, both presented in the beginning of the 90s. Many companies such as Ford, DaimlerChrysler and Toyota also experimented with fuel cells and promised to present the first such cars in 2004. One interesting hybrid came from Italy where the former Pininfarina employee, Leonardo Fioravanta, in the beginning of the 90s, created an extreme sportscar which had rather exotic power sources. Besides having a 231 bhp strong gas turbine, each wheel had a 54 bhp electric engine.

When we entered into the new Millennium, combustion engined cars still totally dominated the market, but between 1988 and 1992 there was a significant change regarding the fuel system. In 1988 carburetors dominated but in 1992 it was the opposite situation. In 1999 all cars, except for a few from the states in Eastern Europe, India and China, had fuel injection. By the end of

the 90s all cars produced in the "West" also had catalytic emission control. This means that leaded fuel almost disappeared from the market.

In the beginning of the 90s four valves per cylinder was a luxury reserved for high performance cars – in 1999 they were very common as well as that many cars had double overhead camshafts. Today many cars also have electronically controlled valve timing which was an innovation from Honda (VTEC). The system with pushrods and overhead valves was since long gone and remained only in the type of cars which came from the countries mentioned above.

One of the predictions for the 90s was that the two-stroke engine would make a comeback. But not as a smoky, noisy and nasty-smelling car like the legendary East German Trabant, symbol of a now forgotten era in Europe.

In the late 80s Toyota experimented with a 3-litre supercharged two-stroke engine and in the beginning of the 90s a joint Ford/GM had plans for a factory which should produce 250,000 two-stroke engines yearly. Still we haven't seen any such engines in any series produced car. There were also great expectations on the lean-burn engine which still is a project for the future. The traditional combustion engine holds its position and will continue to do so for many more years.

One type of engine which became popular was the efficient turbocharged diesel engine. It had such a good fuel economy that someone said that if all cars in the world had this type of engines, the fossil fuel consumption would decrease with 40%.

When it came to the transmission field the use of four-wheel drive (4WD) was rare on a standard car in the beginning of the 90s and only a few cars, like Audi Quattro, VW Jetta & Passat Synchro, Renault R21 TXI, Daihatsu Charade, Mazda 323 GLX and Subaru Legacy featured this practical device. In the end of the 90s nearly all of the big companies had a 4WD in their range of models.

Four-wheel steering was never a hit and was only featured on a few Japanese cars in the beginning of the 90s. It was a good idea but the system was complex and expensive.

In the end of the 80s some companies also experimented with alternative type of gearboxes, among them CVT gearbox (Continuously Variable Transmission). After that it became quiet but in the end of the 90s the CVT gearbox turned up again, now obviously ready to be put into production.

One technological field where development really has progressed rapidly is in the electronics. Already in the 60s many cars featured transistorized ignition systems. Later they also got engine fault detecting systems which the mechanics could connect with a computer in the garage in order to see what was wrong with the car.

Another early device which was dependent of electronics was the anti-lock brakes (ABS). This life saving system was developed in the mid 80s and mounted in a few models. In the beginning of the 90s it was still uncommon but now it was possible to have it as an option and by 1995 almost all cars were equipped with ABS as standard.

Cruise control, radar, voice control and satellite navigation were predicted to be common in the 90s but the fact is that these devices were still too complicated and expensive to be put in an ordinary family car. Most common was cruise control, second was satellite navigation and at the end of the 90s some cars were equipped with voice control. The latter device could among other things control the air conditioner and the audio system. But still these devices were options even on more expensive cars. Another practical device which we take for granted today is the remote controlled door locks.

By the end of the 90s, the modern car was a complex mechanical/electronically construction which, when getting old will be a nightmare for the do-it-yourself man.

Two significant subjects during the 90s which the manufacturers concentrated their efforts on were the environmental aspects and the safety. An increasing number of parts were coded in order to make it possible to recycle them correctly with as little pollution as possible. The use of aluminum increased and in 1994 Audi presented the A8 which had both chassis and body built in aluminum. It's said that this decreased the weight with 400 kg. The use of composite materials was mostly reserved for extreme sportscars which were built in small numbers.

Regarding safety it started with safety belts and crash testing. Then came the airbags which were followed by SIPs (Side Impact Protection) and finally side mounted airbags. One of the leaders in this field was Volvo. By the end of the 90s most cars could be regarded as relatively safe and that also included some of the small cars.

Cars of the Nineties

In this part I will try to make a brief survey of the cars of the 90s. And believe me, it will be brief because in the past ten years so many new models have been introduced and the space given to me for the presentation is very limited.

Very small cars

There has always been a demand for small cars suitable for the crowded cities and for many years Fiat have been leading in this field. But in the later years some extremely small cars came on the market.

Most customers didn't take them seriously but one big company which did was Daimler-Benz who engaged themselves in a joint venture with the maker of the Swiss watch maker Swatch.

In the middle of the 90s the proposed name for the car was Swatchmobile but it was later changed to Smart, which stands for 'Swatch Mercedes Art'. The Smart was an extremely short car, only 2.5 meters, and it was an attempt to make a safe two-seater car which had resembleses with the 'bubble cars' from the 50s.

The chassis of the Smart was of the same type as the Mercedes A-class (see later) and it consisted of a sandwich platform on which a rigid passenger cell was mounted.

The Smart was of course crash tested and the production began in October 1998. Twin airbags and ABS was standard equipment as well as a sequential six-speed gearbox.

Smart had two types of engines; a 0,6-litre turbocharged three-cylinder engine of either 45 or 55 bhp and a turbocharged 0,8-litre diesel engine. Both engines were made by Mercedes and the diesel engine was so far the smallest in the world.

The power plant was mounted below the luggage compartment and drive was by the rear wheels. The Smart was by no comparison the smallest series produced car in the world at the time of writing this appendix.

Italy has always been a specialist when it comes to building small cars. Here are two examples from the 90s; a Fiat Cinquecento (1993-1996) and a Lancia Y10 (1985-1996).

A collection of small cars from the 90s. Top left. The trend setting Renault Twingo was introduced in 1993. Top middle. The Mercedes A-class was a surprise when it came and it was a bigger surprise when it rolled over in the first tests. That was an expensive affair for Mercedes.Top right. The Volkswagen Lupo was introduced in 1998 and was said to have extremely low fuel consumption. Middle left. The 1999 Toyota Yaris was a good example of the new trend in small and high-built cars. The Yaris' length was 362 cm and it could be had with either two or four doors. The 1 liter engine had four valves per cylinder. Middle. The Ford Ka was originally only a design study which was later put into production. It had only two doors and the space in the rear compartment was rather cramped. Middle right. In the middle of the 90s Daewoo made strong efforts to enter the European market. This is the Matiz which was introduced in 1998. It had a three-cylinder 800 cc engine of 51 bhp. In 1998 it was comeback time for the VW Beetle, built on the Golf platform. It could be had with two different engines (1.6 & 1.9 liter) and an automatic gearbox as an option.

Small cars

In this segment of cars many bestsellers are to be found. By tradition Fiat has since long been leading in this field. In 1993 the Fiat 126 was superseded by the Cinquecento which was 7 cm shorter than its archrival Lancia Y10 Fire. It came with two different engines; a 0.7-litre two-cylinder or a 0.9-litre four. The Cinquecento was not made in Italy but by FSM in Poland and in 1999 it was superseded by the Seicento.

At the 1993 Paris Saloon, Renault's new Twingo stole the show. It was a trendsetter and guiding stars when constructing this new car was simplicity, low price and humor (!). Introducing the Twingo was a brave move from Renault because market researches showed that 40% of the asked people thought the car was ugly. In the beginning the Twingo had a 1.3-litre four and the top speed was 150 km/h.

Another small car which got a lot of publicity when it came was the Mercedes A-class. But the Mercedes people could probably had wished for another kind of publicity than they got because during the first tests in 1997, made by the motoring magazines, the new car rolled over when tested for its

behavior during sharp evasive maneuvers. At first Mercedes denied that there would be anything wrong with the car but they stopped the deliveries and started to rebuild the cars. The body was lowered, the tires fatter and the suspension got stiffer. But above all, the car got an electronically controlled stability program (ESP). The A 140 (82 bhp) and A 160 (102 bhp) had four-cylinder engines, the 160 CDI (60 bhp) and A 170 CDI (90 bhp) had a turbocharged diesel engines with Common-Rail injection.

The last years of the 90s saw many interesting newcomers such as Audi A2, Daewoo Matiz, Ford Ka, Honda Logo, Hyundai Atos, Opel Agila, Toyota Yaris and VW Lupo. Many of them were built as 'micro-vans' which was a new concept to the market. One also have to remember the VW New Beetle which came in 1998. It had a strong resembles to the old VW 'Käfer' (beetle) but it was a completely new car based on the platform from the Golf IV.

Survivors from the 80s were the Mazda 121, Nissan Micra, Peugeot 205 and of course, not to forget, the BMC Mini with its roots in the late 50s. Many cars in this class, which were produced in Japan, never came to Europe and the US and were only to be seen in the streets of Tokyo.

When Volvo introduced the new 850, one realized that they had changed course. It looked like before but it wasn't.

In 1969 the Toyota Corolla was voted "The best imported car in US". This is a Corolla from 1992.

Medium seized cars

This is the most important class because it contains what were once called 'bread-and-butter' cars, which meant simple, cheap and reliable family cars. Today's cars are more complicated constructions which are reliable and sometimes cheap. True, there are still simple and cheap cars built for the markets in the Third World where they have to be repaired in ill-equipped local garages even at the roadside. Many of these countries build cars which have been dropped from the model range in the Western countries.

In India, Fiat owned Premier builds the Padmini which is the old 1966 Fiat 1100 D and Hindustan still produces the even older Morris Oxford from the 50s. Rumanian Dacia have, for 32 years, based their models on older Renaults and their best selling model, 1410, is the Renault 12 in new clothes. In South America, Brazilian Toyota builds some of their latest models as well as their old Jeep Landcruiser from the 50s, here called Bandeirante. The same thing is happening in Poland where Fiat builds their latest Seicento as well as the 28 year old model 126.

If the class for small cars is complicated it is nothing compared with the class for family cars. This class contained a wealth of models and some of them were quite ordinary –some of them bordering on luxury car status. It's impossible to mention them all, but there are some which were significant for the 90s.

Among the first new models in the decade was the Volvo 850 which was a milestone for the conservative Volvo company in that it had a transversely

mounted five-cylinder engine and front-wheel drive. Audi presented their new 80 and 100 models and in 1994 the new Audi A4 and A8 were introduced. Volkswagen presented the new Golf, from Japan came the new Toyota Corolla and Chrysler introduced the Dodge Neon which was aimed at the European market. The Neon had a trend-setting styling called 'cab-forward'. In Italy the Fiat Uno was superseded by the Punto.

One reason for the many quick model changes was the extremely tough competition between the middle-class manufacturers. There was an invasion of good cars from the East and the European companies had to fight for their lives. The Ford Escort, for example, had four facelifts in as many years –all in order to compete with its worst competitor in Germany, the VW Golf which also had many facelifts.

Most of the cars on the market were old acquaintances but new makes such as the Korean Daewoo, Hyundai and Kia knocked on the door to Europe. In 1994 Hyundai presented the Accent which was the first of their models that was entirely constructed by the Koreans.

The Audi A3 and A4 were important models from the company in Ingolstadt and the A3 was based on the same platform as the VW Golf and the Skoda

Below left. The 1996 Audi A3 was the first Audi to have a transverse engine and its output varied from 90 to 150 bhp. Below right. Mazda 323 had its roots back in the 70s. This is a 1995 model and it was the best selling of all Mazdas.

The BMW 3-series was not cheap but it was one of the best-looking cars in the 90s. This is a 1997 328i.

Octavia. The A3 was called a 'premium car' in the Golf class and upon introduction in 1996 it could only be had with two doors. In order to make it more competitive against its arch-rival from Wolfsburg it later got four doors and a range of engines from 90-210 bhp.

The Volkswagen Golf celebrated its 25 year anniversary in 1997 having been a bestseller since its introduction. Other Volkswagens in the middle-class were the Bora and Passat.

The cars from Opel have always been said to be good value for money. Maybe somewhat impersonal, but that doesn't matter for the economical family man. One important segment of the class was the 'compact class' where Opel had the Astra, which superseded the Kadett in 1991. A new generation of the Astra came in 1998 and this model could also be had as the five-door Astra Caravan.

The fourth of the most important middle-class makers in Germany was BMW (Mercedes will be dealt with later). The outstanding models from the München-based company were of course the 3 and 5-series cars. During the 90s they were produced in so many versions that it's more or less impossible to sort them out. At the end of the 90s there were 23 3-series cars ranging from 4-6 cylinders and with outputs from 90-321 bhp. The 5-series cars were made in 14 different versions ranging from 143-400 bhp and six or eight cylinders. The cars from BMW were always regarded as compact and sporty but during the latter part of the 90s BMW produced large cars with construction qualities so high that even Mercedes had to think twice.

Some models from Citroën are well worth mentioning –such as the Xantia,

The Citroën Xsara could be had with three body types: coupé, hatchback, estate or sports coupé. It had high comfort and very good road-holding which was said to be typical French manners.

Xsara and Picasso. The Xantia was introduced in 1993 as a follower to the BX and was available both in saloon and estate form. The Xsara came in 1997 and was the new volume car instead of the ZX. An interesting newcomer, the Picasso, was presented in 1999. It belonged to the growing class of high built but compact family cars. The Picasso had close relations to the Xsara and at the introduction many journalists speculated about how much Citroën paid for the Picasso signature. One Citroën model which survived the 90s was the faithful old servant, the avant-garde XM.

Upper middle class cars

Some middle-class cars are difficult to put into the right category because today many of them have so much sophisticated equipment that they are really 'large middle-class luxury cars'. Good examples of this class were the Alfa Romeo 164 & 166, Audi A6 & A8, BMW 7-series, Honda Legend, Jaguar S-Type, Lexus (Toyota), Mazda Zedos 9, Mercedes C & E-class, Peugeot 605/607, Rover 800-series, Saab 9-5 and Volvo S80.

The cars from Alfa Romeo have always received attention due to their styling and performance. Building some nice medium-sized cars during the 90s, such as the 33, 75 and 156, Alfa's flagship was the 164, introduced in 1987 and superseded in 1998 by the new and larger 166. The 166 had a choice of four different engines with outputs ranging from 115-226 bhp.

The up-market models from Audi were the A6 and A8. The A6 was the new name for the old 100 and it carried on with the old body until 1997 when it was restyled with smoother lines inspired by the Audi TT. The new A6 had an all-galvanized body and engines from 110-300 bhp. The Audi A8 was introduced in 1995 and in 1999 it was updated to challenge the Mercedes S-class. Engines were either V6s or V8s.

BMW has always been amongst the serious competitors to Mercedes. The second generation of the 7-class was introduced in 1987 as 730i, 735i and 750i. The two first models had sixes but the 750i came with an all-new V12 of 5 liters and 299 bhp. In 1994 the cars were updated and the 7-class still lives on –but now of course with even stronger engines.

The Japanese competitors in this class were the Honda Legend and Toyota Lexus. Both cars were very well-equipped and showed the world that Japanese technology meant that nothing was impossible. These cars sold quite well in the US but not so well in Europe, where they had to fight BMW and Mercedes. Another challenger was the Mazda Xedos 9 which as an option could be had with a Miller-cycle V6 engine.

Mercedes have always been in a class of their own because there is magic in the name. But at the beginning of the 90s Mercedes were in trouble, sales dropped dramatically and they were passed by BMW. The 'Catcher in the Rye' was the new C-class introduced in 1993. It immediately became a success and by the mid-90s it accounted for 50% of Mercedes sales. This 'small' Mercedes

Peugeot 607 superseded the 605 and was intended as a competitor to the BMW 5-series. Its bodylines also had some similarities to its German counterpart. The standard equipment was very extensive.

had eight different engines from the outset. Either four or six-cylinder petrol engines or a five-cylinder diesel. The most popular engine in the beginning was a 1.8 liter four of 122 bhp. In 1998 the straight six had to give way for a new V6 engine and in 1999 there was a choice of 16 different versions with 4, 6 or 8-cylinder engines ranging from 95-306 bhp.

The Mercedes E-class was born in 1984 and about ten years later 2.5 million of these cars had been made. Mercedes themselves classed this type as a very spacious family and representation car. At the beginning of the 90s the E-class had a choice of eight different engines.

France's contribution to this class in the 90s was the Peugeot 605. It was an elegant car but it never gained any fame outside France. Production ended in 1999 as it was to be superseded by the new 607.

For many years the classics produced by Rover in England were absent from this class. Many of their cars were based on Honda constructions and their new owner, BMW, bought themselves a problem when they took over Rover at the end of the 90s. But in 1999 the new Rover 75 was put on the market. It was a car with classically British lines, a lot of chrome and generous interiors with a lot of wooden panels and leather upholstery.

At the 1998 British International Motor Show Jaguar unveiled the first 'small' Jag since the end of the 60s. It was the S-Type. The lines of the new car clearly recalled those of the old S-type and the Mk II but under its shell, of course, was the latest in automotive technology. Two choices of engine were available: a V6 (240 bhp), and the classic V8 (281 bhp).

In the class for luxury middle-class cars, two Swedish cars had their well deserved position. One was the Saab 9-5 which superseded the 9000 and after some troublesome years under the GM flag Saab came back at the end of the 90s. In 1997 the Saab 9-5 was introduced and it was based on the same platform as the Opel Vectra. A combi version of the 9-5 was introduced in 1999. The 9-5 had three different engines; 2, 2.3 and 3 liters with fuel injection. There was also a model named Aero which had a turbocharged 2.3 liter engine.

At the beginning of the 90s, Saab's big brother, Volvo, introduced the 850 and in 1998 they presented the S80 which was aimed as a competitor to the BMW 5-class and the Mercedes E-class. The S80 had engines with outputs ranging from 140-272 bhp.

At first, the Saab 9-5 was greeted with mixed reactions and sluggish sales. But buyers soon accumulated when they found that the car possessed more personality than had been initially thought.

All in all, the new Mercedes S-class was a fantastic car. The largest model, 600SE/SEL, accelerated to 100 km/h in six seconds —not bad for a giant weighing over two tons. The V12, with its four valves per cylinder and two overhead camshafts, was said to be less an engine, more of a precision instrument.

Luxury cars

In this section you will find the luxurious and the extremely luxurious cars. The Europeans and Americans dominate this field even though Japan has often attempted to break into the field too —without too much success.

Germany contributed with luxury cars from both BMW and Mercedes. At the beginning of the 90s the BMW 750i and 750iL (L stood for long) were serious competitors to the Mercedes 600 SE/SEL, but Stuttgart had a clear advantage over München with 408 bhp against 300 bhp. Both cars had V12 engines and BMW was regarded as the sportier of the two.

In 1991 BMW introduced the 850i which was a luxurious 2+2 coupé with the 5 liter V12 of 300 bhp, later 380 bhp (850 CSi). This model had no similar competitor from Mercedes until they introduced the S-class Coupé, which also had a V12 engine of similar capacity.

The Mercedes S-class was introduced in Geneva in 1991 and it was a completely new car. But it was met with massive criticism because people thought the image of the car was too expensive and smug. The bodylines were therefore changed in 1994. But this Mercedes was a superb car with a wealth of equipment which set new standards as to what luxury really was about.

Among all these goodies you could find double glass panes with air between them, a filter for the cabin which absorbed smoke and other unpleasant smells and automatic door-closers —you simply pulled the door towards its frame and it closed itself. The interior was extremely comfortable and it's said that the sound level in the cabin was so low that the sound from the clock could be regarded as disturbing (!).

The new S-class was a magnificent car and a 600 with a V12 engine could accelerate from 0-100 km/h in six seconds. The first series of the S-class was released in 1998 and the criticism was that the car was too neat. The late

Swedish motoring journalist, Christer Glenning, said in his book *Cars of the Century:* 'One often hears that wealthy people prefer to be anonymous, yet conspicuous in their ability to afford a fine car.'

The battle between BMW and Mercedes will probably continue for many years.

The British car industry had suffered heavily since the 60s and at the end of the 90s there were only two of the old companies left which were still

The Jaguar XJ6 was born in 1968 and completely revised in the middle of the 80s. The new XJ6 looked like the old one but was completely new under the shell. In 1994 and in 1997 the old Jag had a facelift and the XJ series had a very long run which followed Jaguar into the year 2000. This is a Sovereign from 1993.

Above. The Bentley Arnage from 1998 was a completely new model, equipped with a new turbocharged 4.4 liter V8 from BMW. The output was 350 bhp at 5,500 rpm and this 2.3 ton mastodon could accelerate from 0-100 km/h in 6.2 seconds. The name Arnage came from one of the most challenging corners on the Le Mans circuit. Right. 1998 Rolls-Royce Silver Seraph. The name Seraph was defined by the Oxford English Dictionary as 'A celestial being of the highest order, associated especially with light, ardor and purity'.

independent. They were Morgan, but that's a story within itself, and TVR which in 1999 was the largest (!) British manufacturer of series produced cars. Both of these companies made sportscars.

But even if they were no longer independent there were still companies in England which made luxury cars –among them Bentley, Jaguar and Rolls-Royce.

Jaguar had a long tradition of making luxury cars but at the beginning of the 80s the company was on the brink of bankruptcy, mostly due to bad quality and an aging model range. But Sir John Egan managed to turn the wheels and when Ford took over in 1989 Jaguar was a prosperous company. The models which followed Jaguar into the 90s were all old acquaintances such as the XJ6, XJ12 and XJS.

Not much happened during first part of the 90s but in 1994 the 4 liter XJR was introduced –it was basically an XJ6 with a supercharged engine. The most significant change came in 1997 when the old XJ6 got the new 4 liter V8 which had been introduced one year earlier in the XK8 sportscar. This engine produced 284 bhp and 363 bhp with the supercharger.

Bentley and Rolls-Royce played in their own division above all the others. Their history is a part of the British soul and so it came as a shock when it was announced in 1998 that BMW and Volkswagen were struggling to take over Rolls-Royce/Bentley. The upshot was that Volkswagen bought the venerable British company while BMW bought the rights to the names Rolls-Royce and Bentley. How such a tangled deal will work out, the future will tell...

At the beginning of the 90s there were four models from Bentley; Turbo R, Eight, Mulsanne and Continental. They all had 6.8 liter V8s with sufficient power, as the factory preferred to say, but a good estimate is 260 bhp without turbo and 380 with. The Turbo R was probably good for 240 km/h –an amazingly high speed for a car weighing 2,450 kg. In 1998 Bentley introduced a new model, the Arnage, which had a new turbocharged 4.4 liter V8 from BMW. At the same time all of the old models, except for the Continental and Azur, disappeared from the assembly lines.

Rolls-Royce entered the decade with the Silver Spirit, Silver Spur and

The autumn of 1998 saw a new model from Chrysler –the 300M– whose designation recalled the 'letter-cars' of the fifties and sixties. The 300M had a brand new V6 engine with a capacity of either 2.7 or 3.5 liters. The engines generated 200 bhp and 251 bhp, respectively. This car really reflected the spirit which Lee Iacocca had managed to create at Chrysler Corporation. Today the name is DaimlerChrysler.

Corniche. The most 'popular' of these was the Silver Spirit. As with Bentley the models changed very little but in 1997 the Silver Spirit for some reason changed its name to Silver Dawn. In 1998 it was time for a new Rolls-Royce, the Silver Seraph. It had a new 5.4 liter V12 from BMW which produced 326 bhp at 5,000 rpm. The price for the new Silver Seraph was not under £19,000 and as an option a picnic hamper with a cloth could be had for £500.   .

America, with its tradition of luxury cars, lost much if its home market when cars were downsized due to the oil crisis. But at the beginning of the 90s there were still some very large and luxurious cars on the market.

Cadillac had their models Fleetwood, Eldorado, DeVille and the gigantic Brougham, which was reminiscent of the traditional American road cruiser. From Lincoln came the Continental, Chrysler contributed with New Yorker and Buick had the Riviera and Roadmaster.

The Continental was the top model in the Lincoln range of 1992.

By the end of the 90s the market for traditional American limousines started to change because the customers wanted the new luxurious Sport Utilities Vehicles (SUV). This booming market shocked the manufacturers and for the first time Cadillac's reputation as the leading luxury car maker was in danger. During this decade few American cars sold in Europe, but one exception was the sporty Chrysler 300M.

Italy contributed with one luxury and sporty car and that was the Maserati Quattroporte, a model which had its roots back in 1963. The latest version of this model came in 1995 and it was created by the master Marcello Ghandini. Quattroporte Evoluzione had either a 2.8 liter V6 (280 bhp) or a 3.2 liter V8 (335 bhp). When Ferrari (read Fiat) took over Maserati in 1997 it was said that the Quattroporte hadn't much time left, but it managed to survive into the new millenium.

One surviving dinosaur from the old Soviet Union was the big limousine ZIL 41047. It had a 7.7 liter V8 which produced 315 bhp. The last of these giants was probably made in 1994/95.

Another luxury car from the former East was the Tatra T700 which had an air-cooled 3.5 or 4.4 liter V8. As late as 1997, 23 of this big limousines were built. During the Communist era the Tatra as well as the ZIL were reserved for the 'politruks'.

The sports and supercars

This section is of course the most popular in any book about cars because it contains what all small and grown-up boys like most –cars which are fast and noisy. All right, they are expensive –but the dreams are free.

Our sportscar tour will start in Japan. Then we will go over to the US and finally end up in Europe. Why? Well, because Europe has so far produced the

It is said that when Mazda decided to go ahead with the MX-5 Miata project they bought a used Triumph Spitfire and Lotus Elan. The engineers drove them and then took them apart. It is also said that when they were going to test drive the car for the first time, the exhaust system was too silent and had to be revised in order to get the 'right' sound.

most exciting sports and supercars. The choice of cars may upset some. Please forgive me for that.

Seen through Japanese eyes their country has quite a long history of producing sportscars. It started in 1963 when Honda presented the tiny S360 which evolved into the S800 since 1968. The latter model became popular in US but Europeans were not aware of that. The next sportscar from Japan, which became really popular in the US, was the Datsun 240Z which was introduced in 1969. Another car was the Toyota 2000 GT from 1967. Only 360 were made but the 2000 GT became world famous because James Bond drove one in the movie 'You Only Live Twice'. These three cars opened up the American market and when we entered the 90s, there was a firm belief that Japan meant business.

In 1990 seven Japanese sportscars were to be found on the European and American markets –the Honda NSX, Mazda MX-5 and RX-7, Nissan 300ZX and the Toyota Celica, Supra and MR2. All of these cars are still in production.

The Mazda MX-5, also called Miata, was the cheapest of all series produced sportscars at that time and it still is. In a time when all the classic sportscars had disappeared and we were talking about high technology, Mazda knocked the world for six with MX5. It was like the British sportscars from the 60s –but with front-wheel drive.

The next car was also from Mazda and it was the RX-7 –a good looking car– but that was not unique. It was the engine which was unusual because it was a 2 liter twin rotor Wankel. Where NSU failed, Mazda managed to refine this engine type and production of the model began in 1978.

Car number three was the Honda NSX (see page 199) –a car which also shocked the world because this time the Japanese attacked sacred ground when they introduced a supercar which could match most of its European contemporaries. The NSX was good for 270 km/h.

The Nissan 300ZX and the three models from Toyota were also very good but they didn't have the same charisma as the three mentioned above. Another Japanese sportscar which was introduced in the middle of the 90s was the Mitsubishi 3000 GT.

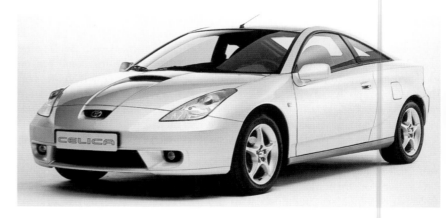

Above. The first Toyota Celica came in the 70s and the MR2 was introduced in 1984. These are the 1999 versions of the models. The Celica had two different four-cylinder engines, one 1.8 liter and one turbocharged 2.0 liter which developed 170 bhp. Below. The MR2 had a turbocharged 2 liter engine.

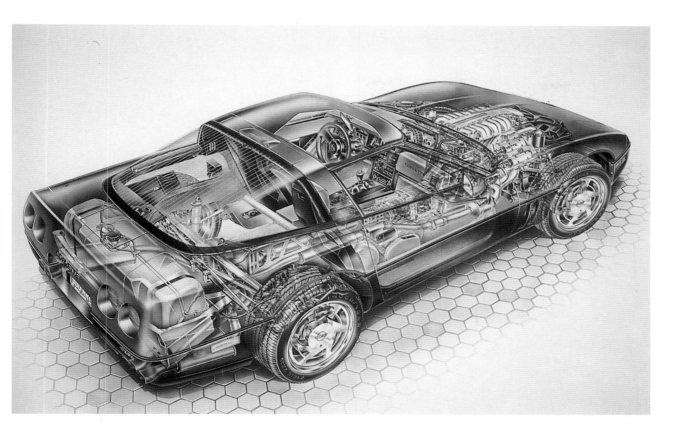

Next stop on the sportscar tour is the US where so many Japanese cars of all categories have been sold. But during the 50s and 60s the Americans loved the European sportscar, especially the British ones, such as the Austin-Healey, Jaguar, M.G. and Triumph.

Their own sportscars were mainly strong, gas-guzzling cars which were very fast in a straight line. On the bends a Jaguar run circles around a Ford Thunderbird. But the Americans learned their lesson and by the time their most cherished sportscar the Chevrolet Corvette grew up, it was a true world class sportscar. In 1990 the Corvette had 250 bhp and in 1999 the V8 produced 344 bhp. Another car from Chevrolet was the sports coupé Camaro which was more like the Pontiac Firebird and Ford Mustang –elegant but not really a sportscar.

But one which really was a sportscar, and which was accepted in Europe, was the incredible Dodge Viper (in Europe sold as Chrysler Viper) introduced in 1989. It had an 8 liter V10 engine with an output of 450 bhp. Top speed was around 290 km/h.

Another supercar from the US was the mythical Vector of which only a few were made. It had many engines but the latest was a Lamborghini V12 which produced 492 bhp. The top speed was said to be 314 km/h.

From the US we cross the Atlantic to Great Britain where so many fine sportscars have been produced. It's a shame that nearly everything is now gone. I will not mention any of them because that's a story to be published somewhere else. But there are still British sportscars left –even if their makers are no longer

independent, except for Morgan, TVR and some other odd makes like Bristol, Marcos and McLaren. Amongst the larger companies which still (2000) produce sportscars are Aston Martin, Jaguar and Lotus.

Aston Martin entered the 90s with one new model, the Virage, which was presented at the 1988 Birmingham Motor Show, two years after the Ford take-over. The other model was the V8. In 1992 production started of an open-topped Virage, the Volante. The Virage had a 5.3 liter V8 with 325 bhp.

In 1993 it was time for the next Aston Martin of the 90s, the DB7, which had

The Dodge Viper looked quite like the successful AC Cobra coupé, which brought home the world championship for GT cars in 1965. The V10 engine originally came from a Dodge truck but it was refined by Lamborghini who at that time was owned by Chrysler. In Europe the Viper was sold as a Chrysler.

a 3.2 liter supercharged straight six producing 335 bhp. In 1997 the top model was the V8 Vantage whose 5.3 liter engine produced a remarkable 550 bhp. In 1999 the output for the V8 Vantage Le Mans was raised to 600 bhp and the DB7 got a 420 bhp V12, once constructed but never used by Ford.

The Ford take-over didn't affect production and today Aston Martin is one of the few really exclusive sportscar makers in the world.

Jaguar was also bought by Ford as mentioned before. They were making luxury cars, but at the 1988 Birmingham Motor Show the company astonished the world when they presented the Jaguar XJ220 (see page 108). This amazing car had a 6.2 liter V12 engine which produced 500 bhp which, with four-wheel drive, gave the car a top speed of 343 km/h.

But the construction was revised in 1989 and now the XJ220 had a turbocharged V6 of 542 bhp and no 4WD. The price was set to £361,000. Production of the XJ220 didn't began until 1992 and by that time the price had risen to £403,000. Only 275 cars were made.

The next Jaguar sportscar came in 1996. It was the XK8 which was introduced both as a coupé and a convertible. Both had a 3.2 liter V8 of 237 bhp (later 284). Soon the XK8 came as an XKR whose V8 engine was supercharged (292 bhp, later 363).

Lotus gained their laurels on the racing track and the founder, the late Colin Chapman, was a master when it came to the construction of winning Formula One cars. He also constructed many fine sportscars for the road. Among them the Seven, Elite, Elan and Esprit.

For many years Aston Martin belonged to the pure breed of very fast luxury cars and the Ford take-over in 1986 didn't affect the production at all. On the contrary. At the end of the 90s Aston Martin was a prosperous company. On top is a DB7 Vantage and above a V8 Vantage Le Mans –both from 1999. The designation Le Mans was to celebrate the 40th anniversary of Aston Martin's victories at Le Mans and in the World Sportscar Championship.

It is told that the late Sir John Egan had a fantastic feeling for putting the right price on his cars. The Jaguars were as beautiful and fast as the Ferraris but at half the price and the new supercharged XKR was no exception. The XKR was so far (except for the extreme XJ120) the fastest of all Jaguars. The top speed was 250 km/h and the acceleration to 100 km/h was done in 5.4 seconds.

Three models followed Lotus into the 90s –the Esprit, the Excel and the new Elan. The Esprit became famous when James Bond drove one in the movie 'For Your Eyes Only'. In 1996 Lotus presented a successor to the Elan named Elise. This model could be had with either an engine from Rover (120 bhp) or MGF (145 bhp). In 1999 the Esprit had a turbocharged V8 of 354 bhp. In 1997 the company was bought by the Malaysian company Hicom.

Among the independent companies were Morgan who produced the same ten cars a week as ever and in the 90s they were the 4/4 and the Plus 8.

TVR made several models during the 90s and among them was the 400SE, Griffith, V8S, Chimaera and Cerbera. In 1998 this Blackpool-based company

produced about 1,000 cars, thus making them the largest independent car manufacturer in Great Britain.

The absolute opposite to Morgan and TVR was the McLaren company which produced the number one supercar of the 90s –the McLaren F1. Production of the F1 started in 1993, and it was the fastest series produced car in the world. The 550 bhp BMW-built V12 gave the F1 a hair-raising top speed of 384 km/h. The cost was also hair-raising with a price tag of £530,000 and a deposit of £106,000.

Before taking off to Germany we will take a detour via Sweden, to Volvo. This company is not known for producing sportscars but back in the 60s Volvo

In 1992 Rover Cars revived the classic name MG by releasing a new MG, the RV8. The new car had very strong similarities with the old MGB.

This picture from the Morgan factory could have been taken in the 30s but the color and all the girls on the wall tell that it's a modern picture taken at the beginning of the 90s. This is an absolutely unique place.

When the Volvo C70 was introduced in 1997 it was a milestone in the Volvo history because it showed that the company really wanted to go up market. It was not really a sportscar, more like the BMW 850i Coupé from the first half of the 90s. The C70 had two different engines, 2.3 liters and 2.4 liters which produced 193 bhp respectively 240 bhp. The top speed was 230-250 km/h.

but this was remedied when the car got a 2.8 liter six-cylinder engine of 193 bhp. Later the Z3 was equipped with the M3 engine which had an output of 321 bhp and a top speed of around 220 km/h.

In Tokyo in 1997 BMW presented a new car in the Z series, the Z8 which had lines that resembled those of the classic 507. The Z8 had a 5 liter V8 with 400 bhp and 0-100 km/h was done in less than five seconds.

Since the 60s and the 300 SL, Mercedes has had a long row of luxury sportscars in the SL series. Many enthusiasts didn't regard them as sportscars, merely as nice 'women racers'. But in October 1989 Mercedes detonated a bomb when they presented the new 300/500 SL (see page 85). This was a completely new car which could be either as a roadster or a coupé. The 300 SL had a 3 liter V6 engine and the 500 SL was equipped with a 5 liter V8. Engine output was 190-326 bhp.

made the P1800 which Simon Templar drove in the TV-series 'The Saint'. After that, the company concentrated on sturdy family cars and it was therefore surprising when they introduced the C70 coupé in 1997. The C70 was a very elegant sports coupé which also came as a convertible a year later.

Sweden is not far away from Germany which, over the years, has produced many nice and advanced sportscars. Among the best known since the war were BMW, Mercedes and Porsche –but there were also some odd makes like Isdera. In the 90s Audi was added to this list.

In the 50s BMW produced a very handsome roadster –the 507 – but a high price and the introduction of the fabulous Mercedes 300 SL 'Gullwing' ended that dream and it was not until 1988 that BMW presented a new sportscar in form of the Z1 roadster (see page 79). It was a nice little car with a six-cylinder engine of 2.5 liters and 170 bhp. This model had an unusual feature because the doors didn't open the normal way –they just disappeared down into the lower part of the body. At the beginning of the 90s the Z1 was superseded by the Z3 which was an even nicer car. In the beginning the Z3 was rather under-powered

The BMW Z3 (above) was the first sportscar from BMW since the 507 was introduced in the 50s. It was not built in Bavaria but in Spartanville, South Carolina. In spite of serious quality problems in the beginning the Z3 was an immediate success. It could also be had as a coupé –not unlike the M.G. MGB GT and the Volvo P1800 ES. The BMW Z8 (left) was a retro copy of the classic 507 from the 50s. The Z8 had, like its predecessor, eight cylinders –but 400 bhp instead of 150 bhp.

The Porsche 968 Cabriolet was introduced in 1992 but, despite its handsome look, it never became a success. It had a front-mounted 3 liter four which had an output of 240 bhp at 4,100 rpm. The top speed was around 250 km/h. The fact was that this model didn't have the same charisma as the rear-engined Porsches.
Below. At the end of the 90s Dr.Ing.h.c. Ferry Porsche AG was a prosperous company and the new Boxter contributed to the success. In fact the demand was so big that it also had to be built by Valmet in Finland. The Boxter used many parts from the 911.

By the middle of the 90s the SL series consisted of 280 SL, 320 SL, 500 SL and 600 SL. Three engine types were offered; a 2.8 liter and a 3.2 liter six, a 5 liter V8 and a 6 liter V12. Engine outputs ranged from 193 to 394 bhp.

In 1997 the time had come again for Mercedes to cause a sensation at the Frankfurt Motor Show –and that is exactly what they did when they released the neat and handsome CLK which either had a 2 liter or 2.3 liter four. The latter was supercharged and gave 193 bhp. The SLK was an immediate success with long delivery queues as a result.

Porsche has never made family cars –they were a pure sportscar manufacturer since the introduction of the 356 in 1948. In 1963 they introduced the legendary 911, a model which still lives on. Other well known models were the 914/16, 944, 928 and the fabulous 959.

When Porsche entered the 90s they had four base models on the program; the 968 (successor to the 944), 911 Carrera, 911 Turbo and the 928 GTS. The 968 and 928 had front mounted engines, and top of the range was as always the 911 Turbo.

By 1988 the 911 had been almost declared dead by the experts but the model continued to live on and in 1992 the output was raised to 355 bhp. In 1995 this prematurely declared dead model was supplied with twin turbos which raised the engine output to 408 bhp. It also got permanent 4-wheel drive.

From 1995 the Carrera also got 4WD and all 911s with automatic gearboxes got Triptronic control which meant that, with the help of two buttons on the steering wheel, you could change gears manually.

In the last part of the 90s Porsche introduced the Boxter. It had a 2.5 liter, liquid-cooled flat six which produced 204 bhp, later 220. There was also the choice of a 3.2 liter engine.

At the end of the 90s the 911 Turbo had a 3.6 liter, liquid-cooled engine with an output of 420 bhp.

An interesting newcomer was the Audi TT which was introduced in 1998. It was a very compact sportscar with a styling not too unlike that of the VW Beetle. The TT had a 1.9 liter four-cylinder engine which gave 180 bhp. It could also be had with four-wheel drive (Quattro) and 225 bhp. During 1999 a roadster version of the TT came on the market. The success of the TT was so great that it even surprised Audi themselves.

As with many other cars, the Audi TT started as a design study (1995) which attracted the public so much that it was put into production. The TT was relatively cheap because it was made in Györ in Hungary. When working with the TT the Audi staff got the order to build a pure two-seater. In 1999 the coupé was supplemented with a roadster.

One odd German manufacturer was Isdera who started to make extreme sportscars in the 80s. It was like the American Vector –a rather mythic car with Mercedes engines. Top of the range in 1999 was the Commendatore 112i. Engine output was 620 bhp and it sold for nearly £55,000.

And now off to Italy, the country which has produced so many classic sportscars and still does. The most famous today are of course Ferrari and Lamborghini. Others are Alfa Romeo, Maserati and De Tomaso.

The first Ferrari left the factory in 1947. The rest of the company's history is almost a legend and the people who run the company today are well aware of that because Ferrari is is the jewel in the Fiat empire.

When Ferrari entered the 90s, production of the fabulous F40 had just ended and the Testarossa was about to be replaced. Other models were the 348 and Mondial. In 1992 the 512 TR replaced the Testarossa. The recession forced

Ferrari to delay the presentation of the successor to the F40, but at the end of May 1994 they showed the successor to the 348 GTB/GTS. It was the F355 which had a 3.5 liter V8 engine with an output of 380 bhp. The old 512 got a facelift and the flat 12 now produced 450 bhp.

In 1995 Ferrari finally introduced their new supercar, the F50. It was a racing car in disguise based on the F1 car from 1990. The 4.7 liter V12 produced 520 bhp. In 1996 the F50 was followed by the 550 Maranello which had a front-mounted V12. Also on the program was the 456 GT, a luxurious 2+2 with a front-mounted V12 engine.

At the beginning of 1999 the F355 was replaced by the 360 Modena, and it was the first series produced by Ferrari which was entirely built in aluminum.

Lamborghini is a rather young company which dates back to 1963. Their most famous models before the 90s were the Miura and Countach. The last

At the end of May 1994 Ferrari showed the successor to the 348 –the F355. The new model had a 3.5 liter engine generating 380 bhp at a high 8,250 rpm. The output per liter was 109 bhp which was a new record for series produced engines without turbo-charging. The engine had five valves per cylinder and as usual the beautiful body was styled by Pininfarina.

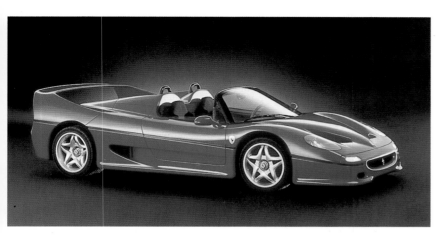

The Ferrari F50 succeeded the F40 and production ended in 1998 after that 349 cars had been made. The F50 was a F1 racer with covered wheels. It had a composite chassis with a self supporting 4.7-litre V12 engine which produced 520 bhp at 8,500 rpm. Top speed was 325 km/h. 0-100 in 3.2 seconds.

Countach left the factory in July 1990 and at the same time the two first Diablos were assembled. The Diablo was a true supercar which at that time was faster and stronger than the Ferrari F40. Like its predecessor, the Diablo had a V12 engine. The capacity was 5.7 liters and the output 492 bhp at 7,000 rpm. Claimed top speed was 325 km/h.

The Diablo wasn't changed much during the 90s but in the last half of the decade a roadster was presented and the coupé got four-wheel drive. The V12 engine had by that time 530 bhp.

There were many sportscars manufacturers in Modena and one of them was the Maserati with its roots back in the 20s. In the second half of the 70s the situation was really bad for Maserati but things changed when they introduced the first Biturbo model in 1981. Several variants of the six-cylinder Biturbo followed and with this model and the Quattroporte (mentioned earlier) Maserati took their first steps into the 90s. One of the first things which happened was

that Fiat took over a majority of the company in 1990. Apart from the Biturbo, Maserati were also producing the Royale (read Quattroporte), Shamal and Karif. The Shamal and Karif had V8 engines.

In 1993 Fiat acquired the rest of the company and started to clean up the somewhat confusing model range. What remained was the Biturbo Spyder, Shamal, Ghibli and the Quattroporte. In 1997 there were only two models on the production line; Ghibli and Quattroporte. Fiat ordered Ferrari to take control of Maserati in 1997. This resulted in huge investments and in a new model, the 3000 GT, which was a sportscar in the old Maserati spirit. The 3000 GT was styled by Giorgetto Giugiaro and it had a 3.2 liter V8 engine which had an output of 370 bhp. The Quattroporte followed the 3000 GT into the new millennium.

Alfa Romeo was the oldest of the companies but for many years their only sportscar had been the long-lived Spider. New at the end of the 90s was the GTV which had front-wheel drive and either a four or V6. Capacity was between 2-3 liters and 144-192 bhp.

One company which for many years led a languishing life was De Tomaso, also in Modena. During the first half of the 90s their only model was the old Pantera which had a V8 engine from Ford. In 1993 De Tomaso presented the Guará which was a mid-engined car. The powerplant was a 4-liter BMW V8 of 340 bhp. The Pantera was still built but now only on order. In 1997 the company presented the Bigua and in 1999 the Qvale Automotive Group in California took over company. At the same time a new model was presented which had the De Tomaso name Mangusta.

MPVs and SUVs

These letters stands for 'Multi-Purpose Vehicle' and 'Sport Utility Vehicle' or in other words vehicles which have a double purpose –able to carry both people, a heavy load or both. Today these practical vehicles are enormously popular and are as well equipped as modern family cars. An MPV could comfortably house a large family, their pets and luggage and take them over long distances. But at the end of the 90s there were alarming reports about the growing rate of tragic accidents where MPVs had been involved –mostly because the drivers had no experience in driving such a big vehicle.

When the last Lamborghini was finished on the assembly line in Sant' Agata the first Diablo was already being assembled. The first Diablo had a 5.7 liter V12 producing 592 bhp at 6,800 rpm. The body was styled by the great Marcello Ghandini who had also been responsible for the Lamborghini Countach. Claimed top speed for the Diablo was 325 km/h.

At the end of the 90s, after many years without any proper management and a confusing model range Maserati was back in business. The result of this was the new 3500 GT, a classic designation from the 50s.

The Land Rover Freelander was introduced in 1997 and was more for the road than for heavy terrain. For the first time Land Rover didn't use any separate chassis but a self supporting body. The live axles were also gone in favor of independent suspension. The Freelander aimed at the compact SUVs from Japan.

The history of these vehicles was described on the pages 109-126 and in the 90s it was mostly Japan which produced MPVs. Then came the Renault Espace and the American MPVs. One of the best known and most popular American MPVs is the Chrysler Voyager or Town and Country as it was called in the US. Today, nearly all the big manufacturers have a Multi-Purpose Vehicle in their model range. A new trend quickly developed of making really small MPVs such as the Hyundai Atos and the Toyota Yaris. The development of the Sport Utility Vehicle has gone the same way, and they are now luxurious vehicles which one can mainly see on city streets. Many people in the US who had been used to driving a traditional American luxury car, now bought a SUV instead. And who would have thought that Lincoln would challenge Cadillac for the title of the best car in America with a big SUV named Navigator?

This is a Chrysler Voyager from 1998. This model which was introduced already in 1984, then as Dodge Caravan, was an outstanding sales success. Since then, many so-called MPV cars (Multi Purpose Vehicles) have come on the market and at the end of the 90s most of the manufacturers had a "people carrier" to offer. Chrysler Voyager from 1998, or Town & Country as it was called in USA, had either an in-line four or a V6 engine.

INDEX

Page numbers in italics indicate illustrations